W9-AHA-883

ISABEL ALLENDE

Life and Spirits

ISABEL ALLENDE
Life and Spirits

Celia Correas Zapata

Translated from the Spanish by Margaret Sayers Peden

Arte Público Press
Houston, Texas

This volume is made possible through grants from the City of Houston through The Cultural Arts Council of Houston, Harris County.

Recovering the past, creating the future

Arte Público Press
University of Houston
452 Cullen Performance Hall
Houston, Texas 77204-2004

Cover design by Ken Bullock

Correas Zapata, Celia.
    [Isabel Allende. English]
    Isabel Allende: Life and spirits / Celia Correas Zapata;
translated from the Spanish by Margaret Sayers Peden.
      p. cm.
    ISBN 1-55885-363-4 (cloth : alk. paper)
    1. Allende, Isabel—Interviews.   2. Authors, Chilean—20th
century—Interviews.   I. Peden, Margaret Sayers.   II. Title.
PQ8098.1.L54 Z47513 2002
863'.64—dc21
[B]   2001056696
                                      CIP

2 3 4 5 6 7 8 9 0 1   10 9 8 7 6 5 4 3 2 1

To Roland

Table of Contents

A Few Words
By Way of Explanation . . .

I have been asked to write a prologue, not an easy task since this book is about me, and more than commentary, it may seem presumptous. The idea of publishing a book that contains nothing more than my recollections and opinions seems strange to me, for I can't imagine who, other than literature students pressured by a sadistic professor, could be interested. So I don't offer this as a prologue but, having been given these pages, I take the opportunity to explain briefly what the experience has meant to me.

Some years ago, during a book tour in Europe, I was interviewed for a magazine. I found myself facing a journalist who gave every appearance of having just graduated; a photographer and two assistants accompanied him. They set up lights and cameras as if they were planning to photograph the pope for posterity, and the journalist—a handsome young man with his shirt unbuttoned to show a gold medallion on his suntanned chest—asked his first question. "What do you do?" Confused, I didn't know what to answer. He clarified. "They sent me to interview you, but I don't know who you are. Can you tell me what you do?" I thereupon fell victim to one of those irresistible impulses, and told him that I was an opera singer. The truth is, I have always wanted to be a diva, and I couldn't let the opportunity go by. For thirty minutes, I talked about my brilliant career as a soprano and about the many times I had sung with my good friend Plácido Domingo, a man for whom, I must confess, I have a certain romantic soft spot. It must be heaven to hear him sing in the shower. The journalist conducted our conversation on the supposition that I was in Europe to sing the lead in *La Bohème* during the lyric season at La Scala. I have no idea whether or not the interview was published, and, actually, it doesn't matter. I offer this anecdote because I imagine that the mischief of inventing another life for ourselves has tempted us all, and when Celia Correas Zapata proposed the idea of a book of interviews, the thought of doing just that flashed through my mind.

Since the publication in 1982 of my first novel, *The House of the Spirits*, I have given so many interviews that it would be impossible to count them, but I have the impression that very little of what was said has any permanence and that almost everything has faded into oblivion. Little endures of what is printed in newspapers or magazines; in contrast, a book is like a rock, nearly indestructible, and that is why I was tempted by the notion of presenting myself in the most favorable light possible. Soon, however, I had to discard such coquettish intentions, because Celia was not disposed to allow them. Unlike the young journalist, *she* knows exactly what my work is, and why I do it. When she described this book as a literary biography, I was struck by two opposing emotions. First of all, I was flattered, since the normal thing is that an author must die before someone bothers to write his biography, and, in the case of a woman, dying isn't enough—she has to have been in the grave for at least a couple of centuries. On the other hand, it seemed to me that I had already said everything I had to say, not just in press interviews but also in *Paula*, the painful memoir I wrote in 1992 and 1993 during my daughter's long illness. What could I add that would not verge upon fiction? I am not afraid to be creative in the account of my life—witness the case of the journalist who took me for a soprano. I have never allowed truth to stand in the way of a good story—for better or worse, we are the legends we elaborate from our memories and experiences—but there is a limit to everything. I can't give free rein to my tendency to be imprecise or to exaggerate in order to avoid repeating myself or to entertain hypothetical readers, because I could be caught out. Many of the people I have known through the course of my life are still alive and could easily refute my story. The danger of a project like this is that its goal is to approximate the truth. I prefer fiction, which is better adapted to the strange soap opera my life has been—with a family like mine, it doesn't take imagination to write novels, I merely take notes—but Celia was inflexible. So, finally, we had our first meeting at my house. It did not go well because the two-hour drive, defying heavy traffic, was too much for her. I offered to go to her house, but since my calendar is a nightmare, I missed a couple of times, and so we decided, with Solomonic impartiality, to meet halfway between San Jose and San Rafael. That turned out to be in a hotel near the San Francisco airport, loud with noisy tourists and elevator music. The taping was a disaster, so we decided to take a room for a few hours, like those sneaky couples that escape from the world to commit adultery in rented privacy. And we rented a room. We would arrive in separate vehicles—Celia with a suspicious-looking black suitcase, and I with a bottle of champagne—and, trying not to be obvious, steal off to our room. Our conversations were always emotional; we laughed a lot, it's true, but we also cried—so much at times that when we emerged from the room our eyes were red and our makeup streaked. It isn't too surprising that tourists and hotel employees would look at us with lifted eyebrows, seeing us as two corrupt grannies; they had no way of knowing the suitcase contained a tape recorder, Celia's notebooks, and copies of my books with her extensive notations, not erotic enhancements. A year went by in that manner, meeting at regular intervals for long, always taped, sessions. By the end of the interviews, I felt exposed and vulnerable, a sentiment not unfamiliar to me because that is how I have felt after every book I have written. In the process of plunging into the depths of memory, which is where my books are engendered, I shed so much along the way that as I reach the end I am naked. This book in particular forced me to delve into the past, to explain my actions as a human being and my work as a writer. I have the impression of having defined myself in bold print and, as a result, having been trapped in an immutable version of myself.

Memory is as subjective as imagination. Where does the first end and the second begin? Each is like one of those Chinese spheres carved from ivory, one inside the other, both of the same matter, independent, yet impossible to separate. With patience and delicacy, Celia was penetrating my recollections in order to explain my work. Her theory is that my writing nearly always originates in an autobiographical incident or a profound emotion. Suddenly, one of her questions would confront me with an image buried beneath a mountain of rubble. That was how, for example, I remembered the one vision I have preserved of my father, and from the time I was three: His shoes and white linen trouser legs stained with blood. Celia went to Chile to ferret out information, and spoke there with people who had known me at different stages of my life. It was truly strange to listen to those recordings because I could not recognize myself in any of their anecdotes; it was as if they were talking about a woman completely unknown to me. Thanks to Celia, who wanted to see all the old photographs of my family, I came across a few beat-up boxes in which my daughter Paula—who had assigned herself the task of reestablishing ties among a clan scattered by the winds of exile—had stored hundreds of snapshots. Where had she found them? I think she must have gotten most of them from the distant relatives in Chile she visited one by one shortly before she fell ill. There, in those boxes my daughter had never shared with me, was the only photograph of my father that had been saved from destruction when a half century ago my mother annulled their marriage and made the decision to erase him forever from her heart and from the family annals. I have it now, and sometimes study it with the curiosity accumulated through a lifetime of wondering what the man to whom I owe half my genes was like.

In those conversations with Celia, I was brought face to face with my roots, which are very similar to hers. We come from like worlds, from tribal families, houses with galleries, ancient aunts always crocheting, grandmothers with the faint scent of lavender or bergamot—only French madams wore perfume—and soot-blackened kitchens where we did our homework and drank cups of hot chocolate as night fell outside. Our grandparents, tradition, a strict sense of honor, and the Catholic religion marked us both. Both of us were converted to feminism and escaped patriarchal tutelage as soon as we could, married men we thought were good choices, had children—without thinking about it, because in those days motherhood was not an option—and twenty or so years later were divorced, again for similar reasons. And as we approached the mid-century of our lives, battered but still optimistic, we found direction in a shared passion: literature.

Our friendship began early in the decade of the eighties, as I recall, when Celia sent the first of her invitations to give a talk at San Jose State, where she was teaching *The House of the Spirits* to a patient group of students of Latin American literature. She was, possibly, one of the few people in the United States who knew my novel, which had not yet been translated into English. I was living in Venezuela, working double time in a private school, and the idea of crossing a continent to visit a place as exotic as California seemed preposterous, but the invitations kept coming, first quietly by mail and then insistently by telephone. You must come—it's written in your destiny, this woman with an Argentine accent told me in her half-scholarly, half-jesting way of expressing herself. Two or three years went by before, in 1987, in one of those twists of fate, the perfect opportunity presented itself. That year my husband and I were divorced, as amiably as one may divorce. We had been a couple for so long that we couldn't think of ourselves as separate individuals, nor could our children. At forty-four, it was obvious that I had little hope of "starting a new life," as we said then, given that a woman had no life if she wasn't married. To escape the inquisitive gazes of relatives and friends, I agreed to make a lecture tour that would take me through a dozen cities, ending in northern California in San Jose, where finally Celia and I met. We had talked so often by telephone that we already thought of ourselves as old friends, and when we saw each other, we embraced euphorically, and before we were out of the airport, began telling each other our innermost thoughts.

I could not know then, but this woman would indeed determine my future. Today, several years later, I have to concur that she was right. It was written in my destiny that I would accept her invitation and come to California. In August of that same year she had given one of my books, *De amor y de sombra* [*Of Love and Shadows*], to a friend of hers, who had read it while he was on vacation and then sent her a courteous note saying that he had liked the novel because "the author understands love as I do," a suggestive comment that intrigued Celia. Seeing that I was there in person, she insisted on introducing us, never suspecting that this meeting would allow me "to start a new life," and that she would play the part of matchmaker. Willie appeared that same day, and we have not been apart since then. I left everything behind in Venezuela to be near that gringo who looks Irish but speaks Spanish like a Mexican movie bandit, the man whom after six months I succeeded in convincing—not, I admit, without some difficulty—that we should get married. Since then I have lived through a lot. Two daughters have died, one his, the other mine. Four grandchildren have been born; we have had love affairs, divorces, joy, successes, and sorrows in our family; I have written several books that Celia, out of loyalty to me, teaches her students with implacable pedagogical determination. And despite many ups and downs—or perhaps because of them—Willie and I are still together because we "understand love in the same way."

Celia and I are friends in the old-fashioned mode. We call each other to tell secrets, to complain, to give advice the other never listens to, and laugh like idiots at jokes that no one else finds funny; we also get together to have tea and pastries and in an hour ingest the calories we've saved for the rest of the month. And sometimes we meet to cry, not needing to speak, because fate has dealt us both heavy burdens, the kind that call for tears, not words. If I had to define it, I would say that what characterizes our relationship are the laughter and tears that erupt spontaneously and uncontrollably, leaving us cleansed inside. It was Celia's idea to create scholarships for low-income students in memory of my daughter Paula; it was she who suggested I set up a foundation to help high-risk women and children; it is she who, along with my mother, reviews my manuscripts, because, since she knows my work better than anyone, she is the only person able to discover repetitions or incongruencies at first reading.

The experience of exploring one's life is fascinating, which is why, I suppose, so many people are addicted to psychoanalysis. Rare are the opportunities—except in therapy or the confessional—in which we have time and permission to observe ourselves, to review the past, draw maps of the road already traveled, and to discover who we are. Usually, we see ourselves differently from how others see us. We learn early on to wear masks we change so frequently that we are no longer able to identify our own faces in the mirror. These long interviews with Celia forced me to stop and reflect on my destiny and my work. Writing for me is a desperate attempt to preserve memory. I am a perpetual vagabond, and I have left memories scattered along the way like torn scraps of clothing. I write in order to vanquish forgetfulness and to nourish my roots, which are not sunk in any geographical location but, rather, in memory and in the books I have written. Often when looking for inspiration before a blank page, I close my eyes for a moment and am once again in the kitchen of the house where I grew up and with the extraordinary women who shaped me: my grandmother, who taught me to read dreams; my mother, who still forces me to look at events from both front and back, and at people inside; long-vanished servants who passed on to me their myths and popular legends and initiated me into the vice of radio serials; my feminist friends who in the sixties conspired to change the world; and the journalists who gave me the keys to that profession. From those women I learned that writing is not an end in itself but a means of communication. What is a book before someone opens it and reads it? Nothing but a handful of pages held together by a binding. It is readers who breathe life into a book.

In the best of cases, literature attempts to give voice to those who are not granted it, or to those who have been silenced, but when I write, I do not assume the task of representing anyone, of transcending, of preaching a message or explaining the mysteries of the universe. I simply try to tell a story in the tone of an intimate conversation. I have no answers, only questions, always the same questions, which pursue me like ghosts. Writing is a slow labor, silent and solitary. Each book is a message in a bottle thrown into the sea; I never know what shores it will wash up on or into whose hands it will fall. I write blindly, and it is always a marvelous surprise to receive letters or hugs from enthusiastic readers; it means that someone has read my pages and that they have not been swallowed up by the sea. Why do I write? I don't know. For me it is an organic necessity, like sleep or motherhood. Tell a story . . . that is all I want to do. Writing gives form to reality; it creates and recreates the world. According to the Bible, in the beginning was the Word. God said, let there be light, and let there be a firmament in the midst of the waters. Before the Word there was confusion, chaos, darkness. This metaphor describes the world preceding the art of language and writing: Everything was confusion, chaos, darkness. Before the Word, human accomplishment fell into oblivion; we could not transmit experience or learning, express emotions, narrate our circumstances, explain ourselves to others. Before the Word there was no history. So it has been in my life: Before finding the path of literature, there was only confusion and oblivion. The written word has saved me from a banal existence.

In the process of explaining my work to Celia, I found myself forced to explain my personality and my actions as well. I discovered, to my surprise and contentment, that there is coherence in my ideas, my novels, and the way I have lived my life. That explains, I imagine, how finally I have found a certain peace. In one session, Celia asked me whether there was anything I still wanted to do, whether I have unsatisfied ambitions, rancor, or outstanding emotional debts. I told her I needed time to think about my answer. For two weeks, until we next met, I conscientiously meditated on those questions, and I reached the conclusion that everything is done and said, that I do not carry any heavy weight, that I want very little, and that I can, therefore, live without fear. I understood that I am still moved by the passions and ideals of my youth; I have lost the innocence I had before the military coup in Chile, when I experienced the scope of the violence always hanging above our heads, but I continue to believe in the surprising human capacity for good. I am no longer naive, but I have not become cynical. I am satisfied with the way I have lived my life, because I do not remember having intentionally done anyone ill. I like my life; in fact, I do *not* want to be a diva or sing at La Scala with Plácido Domingo. I prefer my world of literary spirits. I also discovered that I have made peace with the death of my daughter and with other formidable losses that have marked my path in life. And I have confirmed the most important lesson learned throughout my adventurous destiny, and that is that the only thing we possess is the love we give.

Isabel Allende

Introduction

Though to create you
I must have you.
Your true creation is my word
Valley of Paradise

At the age of three, Isabel Allende entered Chile through the port of Valparaíso, a city of high hills and uneven streets leading down to the sea. She arrived aboard the *Aconcagua*—a Compañía Sudamericana ship out of the port of Callao in Lima—clinging to her mother, who was carrying Juan, Isabel's ailing, two-month-old brother, as their maid, Margara, took charge of Pancho, then a year and a half. Between the fog of the port and blasts of the ships' horns, the little girl in the pink coat and bonnet tied with silk ribbons of the same color must have wanted her mother to lift her up in her arms, too, and protect her from the shrieking of the cranes, winches, and tugs unloading cargo.

Although the child didn't know it, her mother was fleeing the desertion and disaffection of her husband, Tomás Allende, secretary of the Chilean embassy in Lima, whose mysterious disappearance seemed to be tied to rumors of a scandal among the highest diplomatic officials. Her mother, Francisca Llona Barros, whom everyone called Panchita, a woman of great beauty and artistic gifts, had married Allende against her father's wishes. Isabel would later recount the early feelings of responsibility awakened in her as she tried to soothe her mother's pain. During that period, a close bond of understanding was born between them that the years would only strengthen, nurturing with love a nearly sacred respect for writing, along with a need to share Isabel's creative work at every stage, a secret complicity that would carry them together through the best, as well as the worst, times.

Panchita is a sensitive woman, by her own definition "soft outside but with a skeleton of steel." Isabel's readers and public have grown accustomed to thinking of her mother sitting off stage with a red pencil, correcting her daughter's manuscripts, as if that were a running joke in the Chilean writer's repertoire of fantasy. The truth is that Panchita can stand as an artist and writer in her own right. With Ramón Huidobro, a career diplomat—the Tío Ramón of *Paula*, Isabel's stepfather—with whom Panchita Llona has lived for more than fifty years, she has traveled the Western world in the roles of wife of a consul and ambassador, and as counselor and editor without portfolio in Chile's diplomatic legations. Infallibly she chooses the *mot juste* that Juan Ramón Jiménez asked of intelligence, a virtue first apparent in the letters she wrote from Peru to her mother in Chile. Later, she would write her daughter Isabel from Europe, and finally, ever since the political situation forced her three children to leave—"Chile drove them out," Panchita confirms—she has never stopped writing Isabel, Pancho, and Juan, all of whom are located at different points across the continent.

Like Madame de Sevigné and her daughter, Panchita and Isabel learned to write during travel and exile, their literary talent refined through distance and nostalgia. The epistolary genre, private and spontaneous, is perhaps the oldest and least recognized of the literary arts allowed a woman.

Panchita Llona says that when she learned she was carrying her first child, she knew it would be a girl. From that moment there began to develop between them a unique communication. When she first laid eyes on her newborn in the hospital in Lima, she felt that the understanding she had intuited during her pregnancy was confirmed. Along with the natural love between mother and daughter, there grew a mutual acceptance, an unconditional tenderness, "a magical feeling," as Panchita describes it. Neither the inevitable rebellion of adolescence, nor its concomitant questioning of authority—both manifest in Isabel—touched the mother.

Isabel is from a Basque family on the Llona side, hardworking, austere, reserved people, and from Spanish and Portuguese stock through the Barros Moreira, on the side of her maternal grandmother, Isabel. This grandmother, to whom Isabel owes her name, is the ineffable, clairvoyant Clara of *The House of the Spirits*. Among her brothers were poets and writers; Isabel Barros's father was minister of justice during the War of the Pacific at the end of the nineteenth century, when Chile defeated Peru and Bolivia. Through her father, Tomás Allende, she has Spanish and French blood.

Panchita believes that family values are centered in a spirituality based in Christianity, more than in the practice of orthodox religion. Modesty, love of one's fellow beings, sincerity . . . come first. Last come parties, dresses, boys, frivolities. "Just the opposite of what happens today," Panchita clarifies. The values she bequeathed to her three children figure among the ethical principles embodied by the "good guys" among Isabel Allende's fictitious characters.

Just as the three-year-old Isabel arrived in Chile through its principal port, her arrival in California nearly a half-century later would similarly be through a great port on the Pacific coast. In 1987, Isabel Allende, recognized around the world, entered the bay of San Francisco.

"The House of the Spirits" reads a placard over the entrance to Isabel and Willie's house situated on the far side of the bay in San Rafael. "When we first saw it," said Allende, "it seemed it was waiting for us—no, calling to us. It looked a little tired, the paint was peeling, and it was dark inside, but it had a spectacular view of the bay and a benevolent soul. We were told that the former owner had died here a few months before, but we thought she must have been happy among these walls, because the rooms still held her memory."

Those rooms became filled with light after several skylights were opened in the ceilings. Even so, from the room on the ground floor that was once Paula's, you can hear noises that sound as if someone were dragging heavy furniture. Panchita has heard them, and so have I. No one has been able to explain those mysterious noises in "The House of the Spirits" in San Rafael; maybe it has its own ghosts. On a clear day, the house's outstanding feature is the view of San Francisco. In the morning, the Bay Bridge emerges from the fog visible from the first-floor living room with its large windows looking toward the sea, as well as from the ground floor where Paula lived her last months.

To reach "The House of the Spirits" from the south, you must cross the Golden Gate Bridge, that structure of spectacular red iron thrusting toward the sky. Sailboats dot the bay even in bad weather, but on a clear summer day their sails fill with wind and the small boats pick up speed, venturing out of the bay into the open sea. On those days, the crowds of tourists on Vista Point, a stopping place on the road to "The House of the Spirits," enjoy a stupendous view.

The house is large and luminous, its three levels floored with Spanish tiles. Elegant, because the owners have put their personal artistic seal on it, and comfortable because it looks "lived in," with children and young people sitting on the long, white overstuffed sofas and scattered around the thick, brightly colored rugs. In the paintings of contemporary artists, the vases and jugs Isabel brings back from her travels, the seventeenth-century alabaster Buddha from Thailand, the reddish kilim bought in Morocco, one appreciates Isabel's desire to surround herself with beautiful objects. But just as she may acquire them in a moment of esthetic enthusiasm, she also can abandon them without regret. There are people who live for things, who allow themselves to be possessed by them, people whom things dominate. That is not the case with Isabel. She explains that her detachment extends from things to people. She tries to love without holding or possessing those she loves. "The most difficult thing is to let go of the ones we love."

Isabel's artistic vocation—her Chilean friends and her mother thought she might very well have become a painter rather than a novelist—is manifest in her early paintings, in the enormous arrangements of fresh flowers beside the fireplace and in various corners of the house. One floor up is the long, wide, expandable dining table that seats a dozen guests. Isabel and Willie have had as many as fifty or sixty guests in their house at Christmastime. Hidden among the trees, outside on the terrace, is Willie's carpentry shop with its professional saws and lathes; in his free time, far from legal briefs, he has made several of the pieces of furniture in the house and all the furnishings for Isabel's office.

They cook together. Willie is responsible for cooking the meat on a Japanese cement grill "as heavy as a tank" that turns out "fantastic cuts." While he prepares the beef or chicken, Isabel busies herself with the vegetables or rice; she also provides the soups, desserts, and salads. All "the beasts," as Isabel calls them, are her charges, and she feeds them daily. The menagerie includes four raccoons, a fox, a cat, assorted birds, a possum, and "an undetermined number of skunks that stink up the terrace." Malú Sierra, with Isabel one of the Chilean founding journalists of *Paula*, remembers that when Isabel was working at the magazine at the end of the sixties, she was always collecting sick dogs—her own and others—in her little flower-painted VW bug to take them to the vet. "She hasn't changed at all," I told her. "She still identifies with animals."

The Beginnings

What was your favorite story as a child?

"The Pied Piper of Hamelin."

Why?

Because it wasn't about silly damsels rescued by princes. Or maybe it was a premonition. Much later in my life it was my fate, like the rats of Hamelin, to follow a flautist.

Don't get so far ahead of me! We're going to begin with your childhood, we'll get to the flute player later. Do you recognize this sentence: "Life is a labyrinth of facing mirrors and deformed images"?

Yes, it sounds familiar. . . .

You wrote that in *Paula*. What did you mean by it?

Writing that book was an exercise of reflection and memory. When I look back over my life, I realize that I have walked in circles, and that I keep coming to the same reefs, crossroads, and desolations. All those things reflect ad infinitum, like images eternally reproduced in facing mirrors. Memories are not pure, they are subjective, and so it seems to me that images in mirrors are deformed, twisted.

Is that how you remember your father?

1

I scarcely remember him at all; I must have closed him into some sealed compartment of my heart.

You never speak of him. Did he leave no impression with you? No recollection?

The stairs in our house, the legs of white linen trousers, blood. . . . It seems that my brother Pancho, who was only a few months old at the time, fell and cut his head. There was blood on my father's white linen trousers and white patent leather shoes.

You didn't tell about that in *Paula*. Actually, all you say about your father is that you went to identify his body in the morgue.

It didn't seem relevant to me. That's why I left it out, but rethinking it, maybe that's the origin of my fascination with drama: that contrast between the white cloth and the blood. That is my only image of my father; his face, his build, his hands, are off in a haze somewhere. I remember the visit to the morgue very well. I wrote about that in *The House of the Spirits* and in *Of Love and Shadows*.

I have seen a photograph of Tomás Allende: well dressed, good-looking, somewhat arrogant, holding a cigarillo.

That photograph turned up only recently in an old album belonging to a distant relative. It was a surprise to me. I'd never imagined my father looking like that, since the corpse I saw in the morgue was that of a very different man. He'd changed with age . . . or with death. I lived nearly fifty years without knowing what his face looked like.

You have his coloring. (*Isabel has fair skin. Panchita is more brunette.*)

How can you be sure? The photograph is in sepia tones. I've studied that vision from the past very carefully, and see nothing of me in it. My mother tells me that he loved me very much; he used to sit me on his knees and show me art books, and talk about famous painters and history and mythology, and make me listen to classical music to train my ear. But none of that stuck; classical music goes in one ear and out the other.

Since he loved you so much, it's strange that he would abandon you and never demonstrate the least interest in seeing you again. Your work is peopled with absent husbands and fathers. I think your father is most present in his absence. Is there anything about that house in Lima that you remember?

The stairs and my mother's room with the door closed . . . noise, crying and moaning. I suppose those were the fights she had with my father, or when she was giving birth to my brother Juan. . . . The maid, Margara, was running past with towels and a kettle of hot water, but I'm not sure. Like many other memories, I may have invented this one.

Why was there such strong opposition on the part of the Llona family to your mother's marriage to Tomás Allende?

It was a closed, proud, very class-conscious family. Tomás was fifteen years older than his bride, and it was rumored—in scandalized whispers—that he was an atheist and a mason, two dreadful sins in the God-fearing Chilean society of that time—although I doubt they knew the meaning of those words. They didn't have to put up with him, because right after my mother and father were married, they went to Peru. I was born in Lima, in 1942. I'm exactly as old as synthetic penicillin.

You were born in Peru, but you are Chilean. In an anthology of women short story writers from around the world, you are classified as Peruvian. That's like saying that Carlos Fuentes is Panamanian because his parents were diplomats in that country when he was born.

What difference does it make, really? We're Latin Americans. . . .

I can't forget Hispano-American nationalism. Your grandparents stayed in Chile. I imagine it wasn't easy for your grandmother to travel from Santiago to Lima to be with her daughter as she gave birth.

They used the family connections so she could fly in a biplane that looked like a dragonfly, one of the few that carried passengers. The echoes of World War II were barely heard in Chile, but airplanes were reserved for military use.

You were the only child not born at home. That scene from Paula in which your mother and your grandmother steal a baby from the hospital is unforgettable.

They didn't have time to dwell on details—they just grabbed the first infant they saw and ran: me. That explains a lot of things.

What, for example?

Maybe I'm not me; maybe I'm taking the place that legitimately belongs to another little girl. That would explain the feeling I have always had that I don't belong anywhere, that I'm marginal.

But you are exactly like your grandmother!

In any case, I was born in the American clinic because my father had a head filled with modern ideas; he wanted the very best for me, as if it were the birth of a princess. He was very ostentatious: he rented an enormous house in Miraflores, an elegant neighborhood; he bought the best automobile; and he acquired servants and luxuries in order to impress everyone. He wanted to use my birth as another opportunity to show off. When I was christened, they had a huge party. My brothers, in contrast, were born without fanfare, like cats on the roof tiles.

It seems contradictory that you were born in a well-equipped hospital and then your mother went back to the tradition of a

midwife for her other two children.

Why not? Women never used to go to the hospital to have a baby, and now we're going back to that practice. All my grandmother's children were born at home, and so were two of my grandchildren. In the old days, hospitals were the source of infections; you went there only as a last recourse. They even operated in private homes. My grandfather told me about appendicitis—sometimes bladder—operations performed in our dining room on the same Spanish oak table where I write my novels today.

Tell me what happened after you were born.

My mother went back to Chile because the relationship with my father was going from bad to worse. In Chile, even today at the end of the second millennium, there is no divorce. In the forties, the idea that a woman could abandon hearth and home was unthinkable. She was not too well received; everyone believed that a woman's role was to stay beside her husband, without a peep, however bad things might be. Scandal was to be avoided at any cost. "Dirty linen is washed at home" was one of my family's mottoes. Women had no escape—but my mother was a bit more determined than most. She couldn't put up with my father's strange habits, and she left.

In one photograph I saw, your mother looks like Ava Gardner.

Is that right? Bad luck that I didn't get any of her genes. It has to be true that I was switched in the hospital. There's a photograph somewhere of my mother at twenty-five, coming down the steps of an airplane holding my hand. I don't think I was yet two. She was very pretty. She had just left my father for the first time. I was a plump little girl with bleached, tightly curled hair, which explains the miracle of my being born with hair black as a monkey's but having blonde Shirley Temple ringlets when I was one. My mother denies it, of course, but I still remember the smell of the bay rum, the lotion they rinsed my hair with to bleach it, because girls from good families were always blonde. I must have been a terrible disappointment to my family.

You have said that your brother Pancho was born in your grand-parents' house in Santiago, and that afterward your mother went back to Lima to live with her husband.

Shortly after she arrived in Chile, my mother realized she was pregnant again, news that must have hit her like a bomb. She stayed in her parents' house, unsure of her future, until my brother Pancho was born. I've been told that the midwife couldn't get there in time, and so my mother gave birth at home with no help but her sister, who had never even seen a birth and who kept screaming with horror, convinced that my mother's guts were spilling out of her body. They named the baby Francisco, after my mother, and Tomás for my father, but we've always called him Pancho. Shortly after that, my mother yielded to everyone's pressure and went back to Lima with her two children to rejoin her elusive husband. They had told her so often that the birth of a male child would change the marital relationship that she believed it.

The myth of the firstborn son, very Hispanic. There is very little age difference between you and Pancho. A year and a half, or less?

Yes, but recently he passed me and now he's considerably older than I am. Almost as soon as she reached Lima, my mother got pregnant for the third time. As you see, fertility is a family vice. By then my father was away most of the time, devoted to his mysterious travels and his friends. My mother, more and more alone and depressed, became a recluse. My brother Juan was born in the house in Lima, and this time only Margara was there to help. Juan was a very sickly baby.

I don't remember any ailing male characters in your work. I do remember women, like Esther Trueba. What was wrong with Juan?

I don't know the name of his condition, but it was described to me as a knot or spasm in the trachea that prevents the passage of food. As a little girl, I thought my brother had come into the world with a long neck like a swan's, literally in a knot; it was a relief to discover in a family photo album that he was normal in appearance. In any case, his digestive system was not completely developed; he was kept alive during the first weeks with serum. I remember him being fed through a tube. He was so tiny that he looked like a shriveled little mouse. As soon as my mother could get out of bed and make decisions, she got on a boat with her three children, Margara, and a dog named Pelvina López-Pun, headed back to Chile. Juan was on the verge of death; no one thought he would survive the voyage.

It took courage to sail in the Pacific at the end of the war. You must have been about four. Were you frightened by the sick baby? Your mother crying?

My mother has always cried a lot; it's a vice of the women of my family, which, fortunately, through Spartan discipline, I have escaped. But easy tears never kept my mother from making very brave decisions.

The women of my family in Mendoza, Argentina, were weepers, too; it was a defense and attack weapon, maybe the only one they had. Tell me how you tried to console your mother.

I prayed. When she felt sick, I would promise sacrifices: "If my mama gets better, I won't eat dessert for a week." Since I couldn't hold to those vows, because I have an insatiable sweet tooth, I felt as low as a worm. It was my fault my mother was suffering! She used to ask me to put my hand on her forehead, because that made her feel better, and I would be tormented with a combination of terror and pride. Pride, because that meant I had the power to make her feel better; terror, because it might not work. She was the center of my life, my one source of security. I suppose I also was afraid to know that the one adult who could protect me was so vulnerable.

Your stepfather, the famous "Tío Ramón," says that from the time you were a little girl you had a great sense of responsibility. He tells how you used to sleep in your school uniform with your hat at the foot of the bed, ready to dash out of the house almost as soon as you woke up, usually getting to school before they opened the doors.

I'm afraid that has always been one of the fundamental aspects of my character: a sense of responsibility that reaches the level of perverseness. I assume responsibility even for distant catastrophes. An earthquake in Bangladesh? I must have done something wrong. I went through therapy to correct that, but soon I began to feel responsible for the psychologist. Wasn't he getting bored, poor man? I ended up inventing melodramas that had never happened, just to entertain the therapist. (*Isabel is amused, her tone light. We laugh.*)

When Juan was born, your mother and Ramón Huidobro fell in love. It was an explosive passion, but they had to wait several years before they could be together.

Tío Ramón stayed in Lima, and she and her children moved in with my grandparents in Santiago. After my grandmother, Isabel Barros, died, the house began to fall apart, as if it were smothered under a mantle of grief. Meanwhile, Tío Ramón was appointed to a position in Peru, and then Bolivia. He was saving money to pay for the annulment of his marriage to his first wife. My mother got hers with no difficulty: her husband signed the papers with the condition that he would never be asked for money to support his children. Tío Ramón, in contrast, has never, not to this day, succeeded in annulling his first marriage. He has lived fifty years with my mother without being able to marry her in Chile, even though he has in other countries. They were separated during that period, madly exchanging letters. What I wouldn't give to get my hands on those letters!

All in all, it was a most irregular situation for the forties. Was your mother ever able to forget her disillusionment, the man who disappeared and left her with three children?

You have to see my mother in the context of that time and that country to really understand her. There have been times that I judged her harshly because I'm looking at her from the perspective of who we are today. I was born twenty years later than she was. Had I been in her shoes, would I have had her courage? I belong to the first generation of feminists ever known in Chile. She had never heard of feminism when she was left alone in charge of three babies. She was a victim. She had been raised to be a lady, not to earn a living or manage money or make decisions; it was expected that the husband would tend to those things. She had lived the easy life of a "daughter of family," as they said then, and which originated from the premise that poor girls didn't have a family, and then suddenly she found herself without a peso, a single mother, living as a guest in her father's house. Remember, too, that she had married against her family's wishes; it must have been humiliating to come back home and ask for help.

Besides, when a failed marriage came to light, it was always the woman who was responsible for the break-up. They used to say, she stole so-and-so's husband. . . .

Of course. She was the bad "other woman" of the movies, and everyone else—including the man with whom she shared her love, Tío Ramón—were the victims in the eyes of society. She had turned his head. Eve, Adam, the apple, you know. What enormous power they attributed to the woman!

Was there between her and her father the animosity you describe in *The House of the Spirits* between Esteban Trueba and Blanca?

My grandfather wasn't like Esteban Trueba. He served as model for the character, but in real life he was much nicer than Trueba. Thank God he died before he read the book, because he would have died of chagrin, and I would have carried that crime on my conscience forever. My grandfather loved my mother very much, and I suppose he loved us, his grandchildren, as well, but he was crippled by the death of my grandmother. He felt betrayed that she was gone. He dressed all in black, like a crow, and didn't want to show affection for anyone, so it wouldn't lead to further suffering because of love. Occasionally, he would pat one of us children, but he rarely spoke to us, even though he got emotional over the least thing, and cried in secret. I adored him, and was a little afraid of him. He was hard on my mother, but never the way Esteban Trueba was with Blanca.

A redemptive aspect of Trueba's personality is his love for Alba. Did your grandfather have the same weakness for you?

I like to think he preferred me to his other grandchildren because I was the eldest and was named Isabel, like my grandmother, but he was not a demonstrative man. He would have died before he told me he loved me! With my mother he played the role of severe but fair protector. In that family, we didn't touch each other; affection took the form of practical jokes, of slaps on the back that sent us stumbling, and of cruel guffaws over jokes we children didn't understand. I myself am one of those mothers who chase after their children to smother them in kisses; that would have horrified my grandfather and my uncles. It is only recently, following my daughter Paula's death, that my mother and I have dared confess aloud how much we love one another, but it is still difficult to touch, because we didn't have the habit of open affection.

Panchita says that you two have a magical relationship. I say complementary. What do you think?

All that, and more. Our friendship is based in trust, complicity, humor, and, for the last fifteen years, literature, which we share. The truth is that we have a lot of fun together.

Who, besides your mother, spoiled you? Where did you learn to be affectionate? You have said that Margara, your nanny, didn't love you.

Margara adored the men of the family, my uncles, my grandfather, my brother Pancho, because he was a natural blonde, not bleached like me, and Juan because he was good-looking and because she welcomed him into the world, and then saved his life. She would poke milky pap down his throat with a wooden spoon until she forced his digestive system to work. It was a depressing sight to watch, like force-feeding a goose, but it was thanks to her that Juan lived. No one spoiled anyone in that house. If you ask my brothers, they, too, will tell you that we were brought up in the school of hard discipline—but I remind you that that was the norm in those days. Child psychology hadn't as yet been invented. Where I learned affection was with my own children; I had them clutched to my bosom from the time they were born. Nicolás is a grown man now, half a meter taller than I am, but I still have him inside me, like the polliwog he was before he was born.

Where was your grandfather's house in Chile? Talk to me about *The House of the Spirits.*

I can't remember the first house. The second was at 081 Calle Suecia; I think there's a restaurant or store there now. All those streets around Avenida Providencia, which used to be residential, are home to offices or businesses today. It was an elegant neighborhood in the forties and fifties, but then the city began to grow and the wealthy began edging up the foothills where they could look out over Santiago, and Providencia became one large bazaar. Grandfather's house was large, but not as large as the one I invented in *The House of the Spirits*, and much uglier and darker and colder. There was little privacy for the adults, and none at all for the children. I used to play by myself; I made up my own stories and told them to myself out loud. I never got bored.

At night you read in bed, with a flashlight under the sheets. . . .

And in the daytime I looked for a quiet place in the cellar, an area as large as the first floor of the house, divided into rooms with dirt floors. There were spiders and roaches and worms and mice down there. That's where all the works of that old house were to be found:

the pillars, the tangled mop of electric cables. . . . Back then the wires were like an old lady's bun, with strands sticking out every which way, not insulated in tubes the way they are today; it's a miracle we didn't electrocute ourselves.

From what I have read in *Paula*, you went to school in a lot of different places: Bolivia, then Lebanon. . . . The one constant in your life was the presence of your mother and Tío Ramón. Did you finish elementary school in Chile?

Not all of it. First, I was with the German nuns, the Ursulines, who threw me out when, besides being separated from my father, my mother fell in love with another man. They didn't tell me that, of course; the reason they gave was that I had organized a contest to show our panties. I was about six. From there I went to Dunalastair, a rather good English school, but they had a horrible uniform that left me with a permanent complex.

When Tío Ramón went off on a diplomatic mission, you had no choice but to leave Chile.

I was ten when he was appointed secretary of the embassy in Bolivia. There I went to a coeducational American school; the only thing I remember about it was that I fell in love with a boy who had enormous ears. Then we left for Lebanon, where I attended a British school for girls.

Something that really amused me were the games of Sophist dialectics you played with Tío Ramón. When you were free to make friends, how did you get along with the other girls?

Not well. I was never popular. I was shy—it took months for me to adjust; I would bury my head in the pages of a book during recess so I wouldn't have to talk with anyone. When I arrived in Lebanon, I didn't speak the language, and soon I got everything mixed up, the English at school, Spanish at home, French and Arabic I heard in the street. I also felt confused about the changes in my own body; I was in full-blown puberty and adolescence—my hormones were driving me crazy. It wasn't an easy time. But it wasn't easy for anyone else in the family, either.

I have the impression that you have a major talent for acting. Sometimes I think that when you are in social groups you act haughty or distant, as if you don't want to have anything to do with people, but when you're on stage, you change. If anyone told me you're shy, I would tell them they're delirious.

I'm not shy the way I used to be, but I never feel comfortable in a social gathering. I prefer small groups, eight people at most. On stage I'm not myself, I become a different woman; all my uncertainties disappear. Too bad I can't always go around with a microphone in my hand.

On stage you're working to fulfill your obligation to be the writer in contact with her public.

I'm telling stories, and I'm good at that. But in a social situation I'm a total loss; as soon as I can, I slip out to wash the dishes. That's why I'm invited; I leave the kitchen spic-and-span. It's a good thing that Willie complements my deficiencies; he's always the life of the party.

(*I look at her questioningly. She has just uttered one of her glorious contradictions.*) It may also be that sense of responsibility; you feel you're wasting valuable time being frivolous.

Oh no, not at all. My time isn't gold. But I don't drink, I'm never the first one in the conga line, I don't know how to tell jokes, and I don't understand the ones other people tell. In short, a social failure.

In *Paula,* you write that you were a solitary child who made up for her loneliness with imagination.

That question takes us back to the one you asked before, the one about the labyrinth and the facing mirrors. From the time I was very young, as long as I can remember, I have felt that the world is magic, that there are two realities: one that's palpable, visible, quotidian, solar, and the other one, the night reality of secrets, shadows, uncontrollable passions—a lunar reality. And I also sense those two planes in my body. There is the person everyone sees, the one reflected in mirrors, but inside that body, organs are pulsing, hormones floating, dreams and children gestating; memory lies there, mysterious emotional and chemical processes hidden to the human eye. Inside me is the fish I was when I was gestating, the infant I was at birth, the seven-year-old girl, the mother of twenty, the mature woman I am today, the corpse I will be. Sometimes, as if in a fresco, I can see everything I was, am, and will be, and at special moments it seems I can also see that in other people. Willie appears before me as the boy he was when he shined shoes in the streets of Los Angeles, and I am touched by his fragility and defiant laugh; at other times I glimpse the Willie of twenty with such clarity that I feel sexually attracted to a young man I never knew. When I see the old man Willie will be, I am overcome with tenderness for him. I observe my grandchildren, perfect, without a freckle out of place, still innocent of anything bad, and I see who they were when I helped them from their mother's womb and who they will be after I am dead. This, which we can call games of imagination for lack of a better description, I have felt from the time I was a child, when I was still living in the big, shadowy house of my grandparents.

Once Upon a Time . . .

Time total as an ocean,
a wound confused as a new being,
surrounds the stubborn root of my soul,
gnawing at the heart of my security.

Pablo Neruda

During the thirties in Santiago, Chile, Salvador Allende, along with other militant politicians, founded the Chilean socialist party. Allende was appointed minister of health during the term of Pedro Aguirre Cerda, who promoted an open social policy and favored the movement of unionized labor. In 1970 Allende was elected president of Chile by popular vote.

Tomás Allende Pesce de Bilbaire, Salvador Allende's cousin, of French extraction on his mother's side, was an intellectual, a Bohemian, and a dandy. He met Francisca Llona Barros at one of the gatherings of young literature buffs that sprang up in Santiago to discuss the works of the most famous Europeans of the period—André Gide, Malraux, Kafka, James Joyce, Virginia Woolf—and to recite passionately the verses of *Veinte poemas de amor* [Twenty Poems of Love] by the Midas of poetry, Pablo Neruda.

Tomás Allende was distinguished for, among other things, his lively intellect and his sense of humor. Reluctant to lose an opportunity to say something clever, he was capable of making fun of his friends and of crushing his enemies with one witty, lapidary phrase.

In a rediscovered wedding photograph, he appears with a cigarillo in his hand, accompanying a young woman of classic beauty gowned in a closely fitting, long white dress; she is carrying a bouquet of orange blossoms and a tiara sets off her dark hair. The couple seems to be in motion, just starting to walk away. He wears a faint, self-satisfied smile. The bride has a dynamic, defiant air, as if prepared to chase away a vague presentiment of misfortune.

Readers of *Paula* remember the scene during the newlyweds' honeymoon on board the ship carrying them to Lima, when they were seated at the captain's table. And the young bride's humiliation when she accidentally drops a spot of cocktail sauce on the necktie of her husband, who, when he sees the stain spreading, dips his fingers in the shrimp sauce and rubs it into his white shirt-front before rising, furious, from the table. The poor bride sits dumbfounded, biting her lips to keep the tears from flowing. Married life in Lima, and the birth of three children, did not change the husband's strange behavior or mitigate his unjustifiable absences. Debts accumulated, and finally he disappeared without leaving an explanation.

When Tomás Allende signed the annulment document on the condition that he never be asked for money for his children, he walked out of their lives forever. He would die many years later without knowing that his daughter had become the most widely read woman writer in Spanish in the last half of the twentieth century.

The grandfather, Don Agustín Llona, in the austere figure of Tata, assumed the role of father for the three small children who, following their unpleasant departure from Lima, moved in to live with him in the house on Calle Suecia. Isabel spent her childhood years in that large house that with certain changes served as setting for *The House of the Spirits* and then appeared, realistically portrayed, in *Paula*, stripped of the splendor of the imaginary residence.

There the girl began to read voraciously, even at night beneath the sheets by the light of a flashlight given to her by her bizarre uncle Pablo, her first steps toward the "perversion of secret reading." She was captured by the world of fantasy when she began to believe that the characters in the books left the pages and wandered through the house in the darkness. Witches, pirates, and villains moved stealthily about her, and the omnipresent devil was reflected in the mirrors she raced past in order to avoid seeing Satan face to face. She read novels of adventure: she was entranced by *20,000 Leagues Under the Sea* by Jules Verne, and Emilio Salgari's *La venganza de Sandokán* [Sandokán's Revenge] and *El corsario negro* [The Black Corsair]. That is the period when she began telling stories to her younger brothers, Pancho and Juan, just as she does today to her grandchildren. Each one would give her a word, like "squirrel," or "star," and the young Scheherazade would launch into a tale about the squirrel or the star, to the delight of her attentive listeners. So began her passion for telling stories, and at family celebrations the children would sit in a circle to listen to her tell tales of her own invention. In her reading, Isabel identified with the villains; that was the origin of her interest in marginal characters. "I lived every story as if it were my own life," she would write later in *Paula*. Childhood fears grew large with terror that her mother might die and her father would come back to claim her. The mere idea that her mother might marry again created terrible anguish. There was one suitor, Benjamín Viel, to whom she refers in her memoirs, who seems to have won the girl's approval. This is the same Benjamín Viel to whom she wrote memorable letters from Lebanon, ignoring a friend her own age, Cecilia, Benjamín's daughter, who to this very day confesses being jealous that Isabel was writing her father, and not her.

Isabel tells that she was a solitary little girl given to the ritualistic games and complex ceremonies lonely children invent. Her interest in the theater dates from that time when she breathed life into inanimate objects—toothpicks representing different characters—and made them talk by putting imaginary words in their mouths. She also began to paint, following a childish disappointment one Christmastime. Instead of the gifts she had hoped for, the *Viejo Pascuero*, the Chilean Santa Claus, brought her a box of paints and colored pencils. A fuzzy copy of a painting by Marc Chagall served as inspiration to help her overcome her disillusion, and for years she painted "freely, and with unbounded pleasure, a complex mural in which were registered my desires, fears, ages, childhood doubts, and growing pains."

Isabel's great love was her mother. There are traces of the Panchita of that era in the character of Blanca, in *The House of the Spirits*. Like Blanca, Panchita had to work to help support her children; during the day, she had a job in a bank, and by night she augmented her income by making hats, much in vogue in the forties, to send to the women of Lima's high society. On the same Spanish oak table on which Isabel writes her novels in San Rafael, California, her mother combined ribbons and flowers to adorn hats. Although Isabel's Tata seems to have had a successful sheep-ranching operation, the girl grew up in a Spartan atmosphere in which food was not wasted or money squandered. In that family, following the grandfather's teaching, "paucity is a blessing and avarice a virtue." However, from that same grandfather, Isabel learned that it is ignoble to go through life without helping one's fellow man, a theme he practiced every day. Isabel, in reaction to her family's austerity, is generous to a fault, not only with her own family and friends but also with people she doesn't know. Anecdotes abound regarding her proverbial generosity, one of the most colorful being a story told by her friend Pía Leiva. Pía says that when she visited Isabel in California, she soon became aware that every time she praised a painting or some ornament in Isabel's house, her author friend insisted on giving it to her. The same thing happened when they were window-shopping in San Francisco. If Pía pointed to some object, Isabel hurried into the shop to buy it for her; eventually, she decided to walk along with averted eyes and to abstain from praising anything, trying to counteract Isabel's generosity so she could return to Chile without endangering the flight with excess pounds in gifts.

The lonely little girl grew up feeling the social stigma that marked a divorced woman in those years. Her mother had fallen in love with a married man, the father of four daughters, the nephew of a bishop. Isabel writes in *Paula* that one day when she and her brothers were walking along the street with their nanny Margara, someone shouted from the other sidewalk, "Your mother's a slut!" A Chilean friend, Cecilia Viel, remembers that in one chance encounter, also in public, Ramón Huidobro's legitimate wife insulted Panchita Llona in front of the daughter who, holding her mother's hand, quaking, listened to words she only half understood. "Isabel was a sad child, but she had a sense of humor. She was different from the others," Cecilia Viel remembers.

Even today, Cecilia is astounded by how deeply Isabel concentrates when she has a book in her hands. "She would begin reading on the beach and forget everything else." In addition, she had acute powers of observation, and she saw things that escaped the other children her age. "She was smaller than I was," Cecilia says, evoking her friend of those days, "but she had more fire." She laughs as she tells me about one day in the dunes when Isabel wore yellow with a matching hat to attract the boys, who flocked around her. "Have no doubt, they chose her, not me." She laughs with delight and continues talking affectionately about her friend *La famosa,* as her comrades in Chile call her. "I always believed I was different," Isabel wrote in her memoir, *Paula.* "As long as I can remember, I have felt like an outcast, as if I didn't really belong to my family, or to my social surroundings, or to any group." Undoubtedly, she heard the music of her own flautist and marched to a drummer that no one but she heard—until she wrote about it.

Good and Bad Fortune

How many years did you live in Venezuela?

Thirteen, and they may have been the most important years in my life, because that's when I began writing. Chile and Venezuela are very different countries. I come from a land of mountains, cataclysms, Indian blood, and Spanish tragedy, where friendship is a blood pact, honor and rancor are forever, hospitality is sacred, bonds unbreakable—in short, life as written by García Lorca. Venezuela is green and open; it has African influence, the blood of pirates, adventurers, and immigrants from all around the planet who came to its shores seeking their fortune. I believe that the things that impressed me most at first were the erotic electricity in the air, the provocative beauty of the women, and the way men make their moves on them without an ounce of pretense. In Chile, if a woman has large breasts, she wears loose blouses to cover them; if she has buttocks, she never wears pants. In Venezuela, in contrasts, breasts are exhibited like melons in a shop window, and the larger the ass, the tighter the pants or shorter the skirt. Pride in the flesh, sensuality, rhythm, openness, lightness; there everything happens quickly and leaves little trace, as if people knew that our passage through this world is brief, and we must take advantage of it; we are transients. I have a debt I can never repay to that country: it gave me color, flavor, an eye for contrasts, the audacity to tell without fear, and the joy of the senses.

Moving from the Andes to the Caribbean was a radical change, but you were accustomed to moving. You were born under the

itinerant sign of career diplomats, beginning with your father and continuing with your Tío Ramón.

Yes, and then later it was my fate to be exiled, to emigrate. My first move was leaving Lima at the age of three or four, and then I left Santiago for Bolivia, and later Lebanon. I was nearly fifteen when my stepfather was sent to Turkey and decided that we children should go back to Chile to live with my grandfather. Later I lived in Europe, Switzerland, and Belgium. I have had the opportunity to adapt, to learn languages, to resign myself to inevitable farewells. I suppose I should have learned that in Venezuela—it was a welcoming, open country—but I left Chile virtually forced by circumstances, with the feeling of having been dispossessed, of having lost my country, my family, my work, my friends. Very simply, I think I didn't make any effort to adapt.

In your political preoccupations, there are resonances with writers like Mario Vargas Llosa, Gabriel García Márquez, Julio Cortázar, and Carlos Fuentes. All of them were writers who were forced by adverse political situations, at one moment or another, to leave their homelands.

For my generation, it was impossible to ignore the political whirlwinds that shook the continent for several decades. Social and political problems show up constantly in our literature—it's inevitable.

And you have something else in common: cosmopolitanism. You all appear in international publications and are translated into many languages. When you emerged, it was said that you are the woman writer missing from the boom of Latin American literature. Do you feel a part of that boom? Do you think that, among other factors, your fame is due to the cosmopolitanism that has marked your life?

It's difficult—and dangerous—to classify oneself; it has also been said that I initiated the post-boom (to be called the *post* anything is a little humiliating). The experiences of travel and exile do provide a more global vision of life; more than differences, the similarities between peoples and individuals become evident; you stop contemplating your navel and look toward more distant horizons. That gives your writing broader acceptance and allows more readers to identify with your book—which then is translated and distributed in many languages. You're certainly right; that was an important factor in the boom. Before that, the literature of our continent was very localized. Cosmopolitanism allows one to write about a mythic village, like Macondo, but, at the same time, treat universal themes.

What did you learn in your life of wanderings with Tío Ramón? Has any of that contributed to your writing, your life, your ending up married to a gringo living in California?

I acquired a more global vision; I stopped seeing Chile, and myself, as centers of the universe. The world is vast, but people are more or less the same everywhere. With different cultures, languages, traditions, and skin colors, we all experience fear, love, greed, tenderness, in the same way. I learned to identify with the great human masses of which I am an insignificant particle.

Would you go back to live in Chile?

Of course! But since that is difficult, I would at least like to have one foot there and another here, where my son and my grandchildren live. My deepest roots are in Chile, but I have grown accustomed to traveling many roads. We Chileans believe we are the navel of the world; we are always looking inward, studying ourselves, analyzing ourselves, comparing ourselves to ourselves. We say now that we are "the tiger" of America, and we spend the day counting our stripes. We have a superiority complex. Maybe I don't belong in today's Chile, but to the Chile of Neruda that I carry in memory, a personal homeland that no longer exists in reality.

I find more cultural differences between North America and Latin American than between Chile and Japan. Have you com-

pletely adapted to life in California?

Let's say I get along fine. I miss my language. Ah, language! It's like blood, it identifies us. . . . When I go to Spain, or any Latin American country, within a few hours my tongue is loosened, and I begin talking and talking, drunk with the sound of the language I have recovered; it's like a kind of word gluttony. I understand ironies and subtleties. I can share humor and pain better. I don't need explanations because I know the keys and codes. In English, in contrast, I am limited; I can't make puns—I'm not eloquent or entertaining. Every day it is more difficult to write because I'm not using my Spanish.

What is the best and the worst of the United States, your new country?

The best is its potential: in this country both the best and the worst exist in large scale. You can travel to the moon on a rocket, circle it olympically, plant a starred flag, and fall back softly into the North Sea, to the amazement of the blue whales. And just as you can ascend into the heavens, you can descend into hell. I think that here you find the potential for a phenomenon more to be feared than Nazism. All the elements are there: racism, machismo, a messianic sense of history, a fascination with weapons and violence, a superiority complex, isolationism, and military power. The worst atrocities are possible, but also unlimited grandeur and maximum generosity. Everything is a superlative, even the enormous ice-cream cones they give children, which in any other country would feed an entire family. There is no artistic, cultural, ideological, or scientific movement that does not pass through New York. This is a young people—dynamic, capable of great change in a brief time, from social reforms to spiritual revolutions. That potential fascinates me. In addition, there is social mobility; you cross a state line, change your name, erase the past, and begin all over from zero. We come from a rigid, hierarchical world; our past and that of our fathers pursues us. The capacity for renovation and for individualism is part of the North American myth.

Travels

False identity followed your footsteps,
Day after day the hours multiplied
but you did not leave, the other came,
the other you, the other until you left,
until you extricated yourself
from the visible traveler
from the train, the coaches, from life,
from the substitution,
from the wanderer.

Pablo Neruda

At the age of eleven, the solitary girl of *The House of the Spirits* was forced out into the world by the diplomatic career of her stepfather, Tío Ramón. It began in Bolivia, where Isabel had her first personal encounter with Spanish American nationalism. In school, she felt obliged to defend her country against accusations of atrocities committed during the War of the Pacific, which took place at the end of the nineteenth century. Isabel had grown up hearing about the bravery of the Chilean soldiers; she did not yet know that history is written one way by the conquerors and another by the conquered. Small and resolute, she refused to be cowed by the hisses and catcalls of her schoolmates' response to her heroic defense, until the teacher brought an end to things by sending her out to the hall as punishment for her rebelliousness. There, with her face turned to the wall, burning with anger at her humiliation, she glimpsed out of the

corner of her eye the protruding ears of a tall boy who was also pay-
ing penance in the hallway of the culpable. She fell madly in love at
first sight with that stranger who "from the rear" had "the air of a
Greek amphora." Apparently, her passion went totally unnoticed by
the big-eared recipient of her first love.

Of her stay in La Paz, where the air is so thin "you can see the
angels at dawn," there undoubtedly remains her observation of the
landscape and the habits of the indigenous peoples of the Andes. On
the way to La Paz, the train passed through the desert of northern
Chile, through Antofagasta, an area that served as setting for events
relating to the Count de Satigny and his house of mysteries, to which
he took the recently wed Blanca, pregnant with Alba, in *The House
of the Spirits*. The inscrutable face of the Indian may have been eternally engraved in Isabel's mind during the interminable trip in the
narrow-gauge train on which she, her mother, and her two brothers
traveled under the vigilance of an imperturbable Indian who never
slept but crouched on the floor chewing coca leaves. It was difficult
to convince *doña* Panchita, exhausted by the trip and the mischief of
her children, that the Indian was there to protect them; she insisted
that they stay alert, because otherwise their guardian might kill them
at any moment.

In the fifties, Tío Ramón was sent on a diplomatic mission to
Lebanon, where he stayed until the arrival of the North American
Sixth Fleet in 1958. The marines landed to impose order on a land
divided politically and religiously by growing Arab nationalism.

Those years marked Isabel's early adolescence in a strange country, where for the first time she struggled seriously with a number of
foreign languages. Confined with her brothers in a small apartment,
forced to learn French and enough Arabic to communicate in the
street, in a hot climate very different from that of Chile, the girl wanted to run away. After the arrival of Tío Ramón's daughter, her step-
sister who was nearly the same age, Isabel felt left out; she feared she
would be robbed of her mother's love, which for so many years had
been exclusively hers. She attended an English school, and in *Paula*
wrote, "I perfected to absurdity the stoic sense of life." She tells how
she was made to wear a horrendous uniform, a blue serge jumper with

ties, since "buttons were considered frivolous." She survived a diet of English cuisine fit only for prisoners on death row, and learned to recite the Bible by heart and with an English accent. Tío Ramón entangled her in rhetorical traps to teach her the ambiguity of historical truth, and the poor girl, "sweating, but phlegmatic and dignified," learned to defend herself against the ambushes of the word.

Every day Isabel was the first to climb onto the school bus and the last to return home in the afternoon, after all of the students of Miss St. John's School for Girls had been delivered. During the occupation by the North American marines, an exercise Miss St. John considered vulgar since no British participated, the director succeeded in persuading the guards to allow the school bus loaded with her pupils to pass through the checkpoint. This arrangement was repeated every day during the hostilities in Beirut. Bursts of machine-gun fire could be heard in the occupied streets, and through dense smoke, one could glimpse the bodies of the fallen. People fled in terror, invoking Allah; some few unfortunate wretches were hanged from posts as examples to the rebels. One by one, parents began to withdraw their daughters from the school. At the end, only Isabel remained; the bus driver, sorting his way past ditches and improvised trenches, would wind back and forth through the destruction and rubble so that she would not get home too early. Every morning, Isabel told her mother goodbye with supreme tranquility, to the envy of her brothers watching her leave, until Miss St. John was forced to close the school that had to the end remained open . . . with one pupil: Isabel Allende.

In Beirut, painfully shy, Isabel attended her first dance, in the U.S. embassy. Tío Ramón had prepared her with a sentence that for the rest of her life she would remember at moments when she had to call upon her audacity. "Remember that all the others are more afraid than you." It was the style in those years to dance cheek to cheek, faces glued together, "a feat," Isabel says, laughing, "usually denied me [even today] since my face comes about to a normal man's breastbone; at this party, barely fourteen and not wearing my shoes, my head was at the level of my partner's belly button." Her size, as she would often later ascertain, turned out to be her best ally. "It was a breeze for my dancing partners to toss me toward the ceiling, twirl me through the air like an acrobat, and catch me just before I broke my neck on the floor."

Tío Ramón's advice, besides initiating her into sophist dialectics, had a practical side. He reminded Isabel before that first dance to stand close to the record player, since the boys who dance most are the ones who change the records. Above all, she should not sit down or take anything to eat "because it takes tremendous courage for a boy to cross a room and go up to a girl anchored like a frigate in her chair with a plate of cake in her hand."

In 1958, Isabel managed to communicate with marines during the Beirut occupation, despite the fact that the slang they spoke had no resemblance to the British English taught in the school. That was when she received her first kiss on the lips, bestowed by a marine whom she can identify in memory only by the sensation he left: "It was like biting a frog that smelled of chewing gum, beer, and tobacco." How different her reaction to another gringo's kiss would be thirty years later in California!

The three years spent in Lebanon were not for nothing. Experience filtered in as colors, human types and figures, sounds and smells that remained in the subconscious, waiting to emerge and be woven into the world of Isabel Allende's fiction. Zulema, Kamal, Riad Halabí, unforgettable characters in *Eva Luna* and *The Stories of Eva Luna*, were forged from some tenuous memory of Lebanon. The forbidden reading of *The Thousand and One Nights* also dates from that period. Isabel and her brothers learned to open the wardrobe in which Tío Ramón locked his precious treasures: boxes of chocolates, erotic magazines picturing women in garters, and four volumes of *The Thousand and One Nights*. The three brothers and sisters— Isabel, Pancho, and Juan—would steal the chocolates one by one from the lower layer, then replace the upper one; they were soon discovered, but even under threat of a professional investigation and severe punishment, they did not betray one another. Using a primitive lock pick, Isabel, when alone, would take out the hidden book while her parents were attending diplomatic functions and read it, trembling, by the light of her ancient flashlight. Suspicious, she was convinced that the book must be of some consequence since it was kept under lock and key, and that magnified her curiosity. To quote Isabel, in *Paula*: "When I heard my parents coming, I had to close the wardrobe in a wink and fly back to bed and pretend to be asleep. It was impossible to leave a bookmark between the pages, and I always forgot my place; worse yet, entire sections fell out as I searched for the dirty parts, with the results that innumerable new versions of the stories were created in an orgy of exotic words, eroticism, and fantasy."

That Isabel Allende should discover this classic work of literature in a Muslim land is more than coincidence. It is one more among the strange events that mark her life. A thirteen-year-old adolescent began to intuit her sensuality through the person of Scheherazade while living among Muslims and Christians. That adolescent would also become *Eva Luna*, again through the person of Scheherazade. Or Scheherazade through the person of Eva Luna? Eva Luna, a modern Scheherazade, gifted with legendary magic for telling stories and saving her life with her imagination.

In *Aphrodite,* published in 1997, following a long period of mourning that lasted five years, the Arabic world of sensual delights and eroticism erupts like a burst of light in the author's life.

Humor

Which of your books contains the most humor?

I haven't written it yet. I have to wait until my mother dies. (*She laughs, with a girlish laugh that lights up her face.*)

Let's begin with *The House of the Spirits*. The first moments with Clara and the dog Barrabás are incomparable. Some of my students have spent the entire semester studying Barrabás; some people remember that animal better than they do the novel's protagonists. In *Of Love and Shadows*, there are pages in which you move from tragedy to humor without transition. *The Infinite Plan*, however, has less humor than your other books. In *The Stories of Eva Luna*, one finds pieces like "Simple María," and others in which there is irony, but irony that is slightly cruel.

Humor always contains a dose of cruelty. Someone or something has to be the butt. But some cruelties are more benign than others.

For example?

I ended *Aphrodite* with a story that made me laugh as I imagined it, and that isn't as unkind as others that cross through my mind.

Are you referring to "Columba in Nature"?

Yes. It's the story of a deliciously fleshy girl whom a besotted professor takes on a picnic and tries to seduce. And I say "tries," because a cow that wasn't a cow but a bull spoils his plans. . . .

I laughed a lot at that story, but when I think about the poor professor, I can't help but feel sorry for him. You began as a jour-

nalist, writing humor?

I was hired by the magazine *Paula* to write a humor column. Beginning with those articles, I was gradually incorporated onto the staff of the magazine. It was a group of young, emancipated women spilling over with original, bold ideas. We weren't an organized group of feminists, but journalists who were working on a woman's magazine and discovering feminism along the way. My daughter Paula had been born several years earlier. It's pure coincidence that she and the magazine have the same name.

How did you break in, considering you hadn't studied journalism?

Bit by bit. In those days you could still work in that field without having studied at a university. I had begun at the United Nations as a secretary in the Department of Information, where I had a television program. That gave me connections to people in the publishing worlds. Then I went to Belgium to study for a year. When I returned to Chile, I was out of circulation for a while, because my son Nicolás had just been born and for a few months I had the fantasy that I could be a full-time mother and housewife. I soon realized that I don't have the temperament for that role. When I was called to collaborate on *Paula*, I felt like a drowning woman who'd been thrown a life buoy. I was a terrible journalist; I had great difficulty distinguishing between reality and imagination. I put my own opinions in the mouths of the people I interviewed, but it isn't true that I invented *everything*, as some of my colleagues still believe. After the columns I was writing became popular, I was offered a television program, and began to enjoy a certain success.

As Isabel Allende, you became known for that humor column, "*Los impertinentes,*" and for one that was purely feminist, "*Civilice a su troglodita*" [Civilize Your Troglodyte], which must have sparked fear in the hearts of all males. That was more than twenty years ago, and even today there are people in Chile who remember those articles and regret that you are not still writing them. In "*Los impertinentes,*" your forget-me-not appears for the first time. When you began to write, you told it like it was; you said what you thought, even though readers wrote letters to the editor complaining of your brashness.

There's nothing as delicious as scandalizing the virtuous!

Did you ever think of writing stories or a novel then?

I liked writing, but literature demands bigger words. To me, becoming an author seemed an ambition beyond my reach. Weren't authors *men*? And, usually, *old* men?

What was your greatest ambition? When you were a teenager, most women dreamed of marrying. Men could be engineers, lawyers, doctors ... some even wanted to be president. What did you want to be?

Well, first of all, I wanted to get married. There was no worse shame than being an old maid and dressing saints instead of babies. Having children was the natural consequence of marrying. And I always wanted to be working so I wouldn't have to ask anyone for money. A very basic motivation in my life has been not to ask for anything, to take care of myself. And I've done that since I was sixteen, when I got my first job. I've been working nearly forty years.

You enjoyed writing and your column was very well received. Sense of humor, or irreverence for the status quo?

There wasn't any competition in Chile for being funny. We are a people with an insufferable tendency toward solemnity. Anyone who dared to be ridiculous was automatically a humorist.

I don't think that's true, but I think you did it at a propitious moment. Women writers were terrifyingly solemn. I see a more mature, a more triumphant humor in your latest book, *Aphrodite*. How do you explain this explosion of humor following the publication of your memoirs in *Paula*?

As a symptom of good health. I was paralyzed with grief for four years, from the time Paula fell ill toward the end of 1991 until a trip I took to India in 1995. On January 8, 1996, I was able to write again, and when I did, instead of the tragedy I had planned, *Aphrodite* emerged, a book of humor and eroticism.

What humorous writers have inspired you?

I don't know, to be frank. In Chile, people have a wonderful sense of humor in private, but are sober as sticks in public. There was one famous female Chilean humorist, Eliana Simón, but she was retiring as I started. Let's say that she handed me her little flame, because we can't talk about a torch here.

Where do you get your ideas?

About poking fun? From men, of course. They are an inexhaustible source. You don't know how absurd the *macho chilensis* can be. Now I believe that if any man said about women the things I say about men, he'd be lynched in the streets.

I've watched you make an auditorium rock with laughter, even in English. Humor is a constant in you.

It depends on the questioner; there are people with stiff faces that make me terribly sad. It isn't true that I have a sense of humor in English; jokes come out all turned around. I use humor in Spanish, principally with my mother and my friends. In the professional realm, I realized early on that nearly everything can be said better with irreverence. My feminist column in *Paula* would have been insufferable if it had been written in a serious tone, but humor made it acceptable even to men, who, as we know, haven't an ounce of self-criticism. Many of my fans were men who wrote me very sympathetic letters congratulating me for my comments about cavemen machos. Every one of them told me he had "a friend" just like the troglodyte in my column. Always a friend, never the writer.

Humor allows us to see things wrong way round, from an unexpected angle. How greatly it helps to diffuse bombs before they explode! Do you share a sense of humor with Willie?

Neither of us understands the other's ironies, but we laugh just the same.

Not very many women utilize humor in literature.

Because we use ours up just surviving. Men, who take themselves so seriously, can use what is left over to earn a living. Laughter is a stupendous aphrodisiac, and I believe that the combination of eroticism and humor is explosive. That is what I try to achieve in *Aphrodite*.

Rebellions and Challenges

Among the world's effects
I was given the one of doors.
In the light I have seen them closed or ajar
and turning backs
as red as the vixen.
Why was it we allowed ourselves
to be their prisoners?

Gabriela Mistral

When Isabel returned to her tata's house at the age of fifteen, during the time her parents were far away on various diplomatic missions, her grandfather discovered large gaps in his granddaughter's education. He personally taught her geography and history, and when "he found out that I also did not know how to add so he enrolled me in private math classes."

In *Paula*, Isabel summarized her knowledge: "Up till then my education had been chaotic. I had learned a little English and French, memorized a good part of the Bible, and absorbed Tío Ramón's lessons in self-defense, but I lacked most elemental knowledge for functioning in this world."

If we add the fact that amazing things happen to her and that she has gotten into more than one tight spot because of her kind heart, in the long run we believe everything Isabel writes, even when it seems unlikely or contradictory. She herself has said that even if what she writes in her books begins as fiction, it ends as reality. For that reason she prefers not to fantasize situations that are overly fraught with danger—a habit to which she is naturally drawn—fearing that she may precipitate a tragedy for which she later feels responsible.

When she was in her late teens, armed with a good measure of audacity and imagination, Isabel obtained a post at the FAO (the Food and Agriculture Organization of the United Nations) by using the name of the director, which she had obtained while he was out of town. This episode marked a decisive step in her life. "They had me sit before a heavy old Underwood and told me to write a letter with three carbons—failing to mention that it should be a business letter. Instead, I composed a letter of love and despair—as well as one punctuated with errors; the keys seemed to have a life of their own. I also put the carbons in backward, and the copies came out on the back of the pages. [They looked for a place to put me] where I could do the least harm. I, Isabel, began working in the Department of Information." And it was there, by accident, that she found herself in television. Later, Isabel would have her own comedy show, and, at the beginning of the seventies, she became a personality recognized by millions of television viewers in Chile.

Tomás Allende, we read in *Paula*, was too intelligent and unprejudiced for the Chile of the forties. His daughter Isabel, unmistakable in her ancient Citröen car painted like a "shower curtain" with angels and daisies, managed to shake Santiago from its drowsiness with the brashness of her feminist humor. Isabel Allende was also too intelligent and unprejudiced for the society of her time. She did not accept that there should be different rules for women and men. She did not tolerate a double standard either in thought or in work.

In her column for the magazine *Paula,* Isabel, ingeniously playful and bold, focused on the eternal battle of the sexes from a feminist point of view: "Just for the fun of shocking everyone, I would have marched through the streets with a bra impaled on a broomstick." She needed a good dose of courage to confront Chile during the sixties. "The prudish and moralistic atmosphere, the small-town mentality, and the rigidity of Chilean social norms at that time were overpowering."

As a journalist, she questioned everything that was institutionally sacred. Soap operas, political farce, the Latin male's infidelity, the mercenary tone of Christmas, family vacations at the beach, beauty treatments, and even aphrodisiac recipes for seducing a man, appeared in her weekly column, altering the provincial peace of Santiago.

In 1967, in the fifth issue of *Paula*, Isabel Allende summarized man's journey from the cave to the twentieth century, passing waggishly through various historical ages. Three examples will illustrate her humor. "The man of the Roman empire devoted himself to orgies and to killing Christians. These orgies were responsible for the demographic explosion and the development of the viticulture industry. . . . The Renaissance man was gallant; he picked up his beloved's handkerchief but did not blow his nose in it. He died of tuberculosis, of love, or in a duel. . . . Twentieth-century man lives in cement mousetraps, eats canned fruit, buys on credit, plans his family, drives a van, and believes in statistics. He is born without pain, lives a life of boredom, and dies of cancer."

In her column on the modern Don Juan, the journalist warned her readers: "He is a lover by vocation, a conqueror that goes around collecting women like a philatelist collects stamps. We learn to know him, to understand him, and to resist him." She recognized eight types of Don Juans. Let's consider the last on the list. "The mature Don Juan; he has passed the mid-century mark but walks with his stomach sucked in, radiating energy and charm. He steps inside his house and shrivels like a balloon, puts on his bedroom slippers, and takes his blood pressure."

She also laughed at husbands, whom she classifies as follows: the American husband, So-and-So's husband, husband who loves his wife (fifties film husband), unfaithful husband, elegant husband, affectionate husband, henpecked husband, ideal husband, Latin husband, and vacation husband. Of the next-to-last, she wrote: "Do not confuse the Latin husband with the Latin lover, his antithesis. These husbands vary according to whether they are Mexican, Italian, Bolivian, Cuban, or Chilean. The common factor is that they covet their neighbor's wife."

With one swift sweep of the pen, half-joking, half-sincere, Isabel challenged the machismo rampant in Latin American societies, along with the social practices that were not discussed, but tacitly accepted. Seditious and iconoclastic, she set out to stir the hornet's nest in the sixties by ridiculing everyone. Even though letters to the editor threatened a horrible fate, the author of these feminist diatribes enjoyed the company of a man, her husband Miguel Frías, who loved her, respected her, and did not interfere in her work. Isabel was the only one of the editorial staff of *Paula* who survives Chilean society's attacks on feminism. Her co-workers all divorced in the seventies. In the dedication of *Civilice a su troglodita*, she says: "This book is dedicated with love to those who inspired it: men in general, and one in particular (Miguel Frías)."

Because of her irrepressible sense of humor, Isabel could not resist the temptation to make a joke when the opportunity presented itself. Without intending it, she ended up being as corrosive as Tomás Allende, her father, satirizing theater and television programs so effectively that they were cancelled. Looking back, Isabel regrets some of her early humorous criticism and its devastating consequences. "To make a joke, I was capable of destroying someone. I wouldn't do that again, I will regret it for the rest of my life."

Nevertheless, she has not been cured of her boldness. In March of 1994, at the Palacio de La Moneda where her uncle Salvador Allende died twenty-one years earlier, in a solemn ceremony in which she accepted the Gabriela Mistral prize from the hands of President Patricio Aylwin, Isabel said: "I suppose that most women are comfortable being female. It took me four decades to accept being a woman; before that, I had always wanted to be a man. It wasn't a case of Freudian envy, you can be sure. What's to envy about a capricious little appendage? Frankly, if I had one, I wouldn't know where to put it. Oh, forgive me, *Señor Presidente*, I'm speaking in general terms; I'm not referring to anyone in particular."

Isabel has said about her articles from that feminist epoch: "If any man dared write about the opposite sex with equal insolence, he would be lynched in a public plaza by a throng of enraged women, but no one took me seriously."

Even today she likes to scandalize men in her lectures. On one occasion at my university, a man who had come to hear her asked me, confused, "Why does she attack men that way?" And I answered, "Because she loves them so much."

The theme of eroticism inspired her to write *Aphrodite*, published in Spanish in 1997 and in English in 1998. In this work, the aphrodisiac recipes are bona fide; they work, the author guarantees. It would have been interesting to have included a recipe that appeared in *Civilice a su troglodita* twenty-three years earlier. Its author reports that it is from the *Gran libro de San Cipriano* [The Large Book of St. Cyprian] and that it is "simple and cheap." Here it is in its entirety.

"Take a flax seed and crush it in a marble pestle. Add the left testicle of a four-year-old black goat and a pinch of powders obtained from hair from the back of a white dog, cut the first day of the new moon and burned seven days afterward. All these ingredients should be set to steep in a flask half filled with good liquor and left, unsealed, for twenty-one days, exposed to the influence of the planets. At the end of this period, cook until the mixture is reduced to the consistency of thin oatmeal. Strain and rub the liquid on the male parts."

By way of warning, the author adds: "It is possible that you will be unable to find all these ingredients in the supermarket, but [s]he who seeks, shall find. Similarly, it is not clear on what parts this recipe should be rubbed, so we recommend that you double the recipe and apply over the entire body."

When Isabel attacked the soap opera *La Gata* [The Cat] in her column, public reaction was ferocious. In a letter to the editor, Carmen Gómez de Rancagua said, among other things, that "an article by Isabel Allende on the subject of *La Gata* was not favorably received by avid readers of the magazine. She speaks of a carnival. . . . The journalist reveals her envy of the triumph of this cast, perhaps because she herself would like to work in television. . . . I find no reason why my children should not watch *La Gata*, but I do not allow them to read this writer's articles, and I turned off the television when she appeared on a segment of *Buenas noches.* I would not allow my children to listen to her." A male reader angrily railed against her, warning that she should stop writing the column *Civilice a su troglodita* if she did not want to become the "laughingstock of Santiago." The letter assumed that she wrote the way she did because she was a spinster and desperate to find a husband. His rage was so consuming that his last counsel was "Fight against your complex or your failed life. Good luck. P.S. I challenge you to publish this letter, unedited, in *Paula.* You have succeeded in making me loathe you with all my heart. Yours truly, Max M.M., Santiago."

In the meantime, Isabel, happily married and the mother of two children, lived a fulfilled life as adviser to the "Lonely Hearts Column," helping lovers achieve a tender reconciliation. She wrote under the pseudonym of Francisca Román, a name inspired by her mother, Francisca, and her stepfather, Ramón. She interviewed murderers, drug addicts, and prostitutes, as well as politicians and entrepreneurs on her television program, supporting her family with her colossal energy, and practicing a lukewarm feminism, taking upon her shoulders the man's responsibilities without assuming any of his rights.

On the eve of leaving Chile for exile in Venezuela, profoundly affected by the military coup of 1973, Isabel wrote one of her last humor columns for *Paula,* attacking to the limits permitted by military censorship the corruption spreading throughout Chile. In April 1974, she wrote this column entitled "Pirates."

"Pirates do not have to earn their living by the sweat of their brow; they earn it with other people's. They reach out a hand—the one holding a pistol—and appropriate their victims' earnings. When I was young I believed that pirates were people who stumped around with a wooden leg and a patch over one eye, but now I know some who wear suits by Juvens and shoes by Jarman. When they are satisfied with their accumulated treasures, they become politicians and settle down to govern . . . at least until something unexpected happens and they find themselves, as in Chile, frustrated in their wishes." The allusion is clear, and it will have a backlash.

The House of the Spirits

I am interested to know the connection between the characters in this novel and the flesh-and-blood people who lived with you. Does your uncle resemble the Marcos of *The House of the Spirits*?

There are two characters in *The House of the Spirits* based on Marcos. In real life he was indescribable.

And your other uncle?

The character of Jaime is based on my uncle Pablo, although in real life he wasn't murdered, as I tell in the book. He died in an accident. He was in a small plane crossing the desert of Atacama, in northern Chile, when the engine exploded in midair. There was nothing left. . . . I still remember my grandfather's face when they gave him the news: a mask of stone. He didn't shed a single tear, and he never again spoke the name of that adored son, his favorite, his confidante and friend. We were stoics, following the example set by my grandfather. And grief was something very private. My grandfather would never have approved the public exhibition of suffering in *Paula*. Uncle Pablo was not a physician, like Jaime, nor was he involved in politics, but he was a person defeated by his good heart, always concerned with helping others, a friend of any forlorn soul who crossed his path, just like Jaime.

It appears that your uncles were important to your childhood.

With relatives like them, I didn't have to invent anything; they met all the requisites for magical realism. Mine was a family of men: grandfather, uncles, brothers. In *Paula,* I described their rough games: pushing children to the limit to make them strong. If we survived that, we could handle anything. There were no modern theories on child psychology; childhood was not a happy time. To the contrary, it was your misfortune to be a child, and the one consolation was that you grew out of it. My uncles did not make my life easy; all they did was pester me.

Your childhood differs in certain aspects from Alba's, but in age and personality, she is the character you resemble most closely.

None of the characters in *The House of the Spirits* is exactly like any of my family, except maybe Clara. She was like the grandmother I remember and have been told about, though slightly exaggerated. It isn't true that she could play the piano with the lid closed; she never learned to play at all. Esteban Trueba is based on my grandfather, but I altered his biography and embroidered his defects. The Candidate—later called the President—is, of course, Salvador Allende; the Poet is Pablo Neruda; and the inspiration for Pedro Tercero García is Víctor Jara, the militant singer who was tortured and murdered in the Estadio Nacional, which was turned into a prison during the first days of the military coup of 1973.

I see in you, in your life and in your work, a great sense of social concern. It is one of the things that stands out most. I confess that at first what I liked best, like everyone else, was the plot, your ability to move so quickly from one situation to the next, whetting the reader's appetite for the denouement—which, after all, is what a great narrator does. It was later that I began to be aware of the emphasis on what I would call a social conscience. What was happening in the Chilean political arena during that time, and how do you explain the origin of your social conscience? Was it solely the influence of certain members of your family, or did some external element activate you?

Social injustice is so oppressive in Latin America that only a cretin could fail to see it. I was aware of it as soon as I could think.

But it wasn't a subject discussed in my family. When I say that I come from a very political family, I'm referring to the Allendes, and later to the family formed by my mother and stepfather. But in my grandfather's home, a conservative climate ruled; no one was politicized. In their minds, economic and social differences were natural, part of the divine order. They did, nevertheless, have a desire to help the poor, something my grandmother instilled more out of a sense of Christian charity than social justice. Instinctively, however, I always knew that charity is humiliating to the person who receives it. From an early age I rebelled against the system of social classes, against the way the servants were treated, against the way the rooms occupied by the family were divided—like crossing an invisible frontier—from the dark regions of the patios, the kitchen, the maids' rooms, all the places that we children inhabited. José Donoso masterfully described that in his novels. The living room, the dining room, the library, were always impeccable, but the kitchen was a pigpen. The maids' rooms were dark, unhealthy caves. Our house was no exception; they were all like that—no one questioned it. I, however, always felt it as a personal affront.

When you introduce Nívea in *The House of the Spirits*, even though you never give a perceptible chronological clue, you present her as thoroughly informed about early feminism in Chile, and you invest her with a social conscience that doesn't appear in other female characters until Alba. What period was that in Chile? The early twentieth century?

Nívea had to have lived at the end of the last century and beginnings of the twentieth, when the suffragists were still marching in corsets, long skirts, and long hair, and chaining themselves to the iron gates of the Congress, to the stupor of their own husbands. In Europe and North America, women were fighting for the vote, convinced that once they got it, everything else would fall into place. In Chile, the suffragists came primarily from the upper social classes, in which a few women were educated and had access to information. In that novel, Clara, too, has a social conscience. Do you remember her harangues to the campesinos?

Of course I do. Was there anyone in your home who resembled Nívea? Because we've agreed that Clara had your grandmother's sweetness.

No, not that I'm aware of.

You've said that you began *The House of the Spirits* as a long letter to your grandfather. How is it that, at the beginning, a character appears who is so foreign to a Chilean upper-middle-class family? A woman with a lot of children who still has time for social work? My impression is that the first part of the novel is a fantasy based on Chilean historical reality, but that it's over the edge until Esteban Trueba enters with a different attitude. The beginning, with Padre Restrepo's heated sermon, sets the tone.

Nívea actually wasn't unusual; nearly all women of that day, including the suffragists, had a large number of children. Father Restrepo actually existed, and his sermons were just as they are in the novel; I didn't have to invent them. With his tongue, that priest could strike fear into the bravest heart.

The novel begins with a burst of impassioned madness. You put yourself in Nívea's corset, and the reader is immediately drawn in. I don't know whether you meant to be realistic or whether you were practicing your innate sense of humor, that tendency you have for stepping over the edge, for exaggeration, and laughter.

When I began *The House of the Spirits*, I was writing for my grandfather—well, more accurately, for the ghost of my grandfather. I wrote the first sentence: *Barrabás came to us by sea*, and the only thing I knew was that Barrabás was a dog, because we had one by that name. Everything else followed from there. And I went way back and, as you say, my imagination overflowed; I wanted to write about my grandparents, but I was betrayed by my eagerness to tell a story. Why did I start with Nívea? I don't know. You ask if it was a conscious use of humor . . . I had no awareness of anything. *The House of the Spirits* was like opening a floodgate; a torrent of words, histories, stories, images, colors, tastes, and memories roared down, swept me off my feet, and I've been head over heels to this very day. I never recovered from the tremendous impact of that torrent. It changed my life.

Didn't you have a script, an outline for the book?

I didn't make an outline; I wrote in great outpourings. The truth is that I always write blindly. I'm incapable of following a plan. When I finished the book, there were characters that hadn't grown a day older; seventy years of history had gone by and they were still eighteen. You can't imagine the contradictions, the errors of time and place. My husband then, Miguel Frías, who is an engineer, made a kind of chart and pinned it on the wall so that I could follow the lives of the characters and periods. Everything was a jumble; I needed someone with a mathematical mentality to untangle the story. You ask me to tell you what I intended; I confess I didn't have a plan, nothing but a desire to tell a story.

Might we say that the book was an explosion of creativity, something you had stored up in your subconscious, and when released, it came roaring out, rolling before it the story of a family that exile defined from afar?

Exactly. In trying to reclaim the members of my family, I ended up writing something that didn't resemble them. The book was based on the life of my family and on the history of Chile, but it was more fiction than reality. Several relatives stopped speaking to me, but with time they've become reconciled to the novel, and it's now become the official history of the family.

I know a professor who has studied the book in great detail, and after charting what happened, page by page, he verified that it coincides exactly with historical events in Chile. The earthquake, the political and social situations, all gave him a frame for setting precise dates for each chapter.

You certainly don't think that was accidental!

The House of the Spirits **is your most expansive book. Let's look**

at the process of its creation.

It took a year, writing only at night. I was working twelve hours a day at a school. From seven in the morning to one in the elementary grades, and from one to seven in the secondary school. I didn't even have a half hour for lunch. At night I went home, which fortunately was close by, ate dinner with my family, showered with soap and water to wash away the fatigue of the day, and sat down to write until I couldn't stay awake. We were living on the second floor of a house in Las Colinas de Bello Monte in Caracas, Venezuela. The house was on a steep hill; it had a great view of the city. Our landlady lived downstairs, and we up. It was a very ugly house, but comfortable, well located, and easy to clean. At first I wrote in the dining room after the family ate dinner, but since the television was in that room, I soon moved into the kitchen. Toward the end, I set up a table in the bedroom.

Miguel wasn't there?

He was, but he didn't care. Just the opposite, I think he was very happy; that way I wasn't a worry. I've noticed that when I'm not busy, my family gets nervous. . . .

I suppose that the children were asleep, too, and that the next morning the one person suffering from staying up late was you.

The writing was like a drug that kept me alert, awake, strong, and healthy. It still is; when I'm not writing, I get fat.

Did you read what you were writing to anyone during that period?

I never do that. I don't like to show my work before it's finished; it's like walking around in my underwear. Why showed my cellulitis if I look much better in stockings? At the end I showed the manuscript to my mother. Her first reaction when she read *The House of the Spirits* was one of horror. When she came to the part about the Conde de Satigny, she said, "How can you tell those things about your father? You even called him by name!" I realized then that my worst fantasies about my father were true. In the first version, the count was named Bilbaire. I didn't know, or I hadn't remembered, that one of my father's surnames was Bilbaire. Maybe I'd heard it sometime in my childhood and buried it, but when I named the character, I wasn't aware of the similarity. Haven't I said this in *Paula* or somewhere? It sounds like ancient history to me.

Don't worry. Repetitions in these things are inevitable. You said that Miguel put your characters on a chart, something like a family tree. When did he do that?

When the book was finished, after my mother corrected it, and he and Paula had read it.

I see there is no one named Bilbaire . . .

At my mother's request, I had to change the name. And I had to choose one with more or less the same number of letters. I used Typex to white out *Bilbaire*, rolled every page back in the typewriter, and typed the new name in the space. That's why I chose *Satigny*. We had a tray that had a map of France on it, and I discovered a place with that name.

What a strange phenomenon of subconscious memory that a child would hear something, forget it, keep it for the day she needed it or wanted to remember. It's like money deposited in the bank.

My mother was the first to say "This reads like a novel." She corrected the language and gave me some ideas about form. Miguel, and Paula, who was barely seventeen, analyzed the plot, identified the errors and inconsistencies. I had to change everything from the earthquake on, because the dates and the ages of the characters and the period didn't coincide with Chilean history. It was like putting the story in a straightjacket.

I wonder whether you fully realized what you had done, whether you thought you were going to be a great writer. Did you imagine that ever?

Of course not! How could I know I would be that lucky? I've always been drawn to telling stories. I used to be called a liar; now that I earn my living with lies, it turns out I'm a writer.

What did you decide to do once you had finished the manuscript of *The House of the Spirits?*

My mother, who has much more spunk than I do, sent it to an editor, a friend of hers, but the answer was negative. We tried it several different places, but got no response. I knew a Chilean editor in Caracas, who also rejected it, but his assistant, who was an exiled journalist, told me she had read the manuscript and thought it had possibilities. She suggested I get a literary agent.

Do you think the fact that it was written by a woman had anything to do with the initial negative reaction?

Of course. I still meet men who announce proudly that they don't read literature written by "girls." Only recently a letter came to me from a woman who studies literature in Mexico whose professor had forbidden her to read my books because he thinks they're "light" literature, and he makes fun of poems by his women students, calling them "ovarian excrescence."

Those editors who rejected *The House of the Spirits*—did they at least read it?

I have no idea.

You have told me that Carmen Balcells made a deal with Plaza y Janés in Spain. She offered to give them the book of a well-known author if they also accepted yours, isn't that true?

I don't remember her exact strategy, but it was something like that. My book came out riding the tail of a contract with a famous writer. That same year my novel was the buzz at the Frankfurt Book Fair. Word got around, and all the European publishers were interested. The first translation contract was with Fayard in France, then

Germany, the Scandinavian countries, Italy, and so on.

What was the first printing of your novel?

I haven't any idea, but I suppose Carmen has the figures.

Do you remember the first cover?

It was pink, with a woman with green hair, horrible, but I thought it was wonderful. Tío Ramón contacted a diplomat friend in the Chilean Embassy in Spain, who sent us the first copies by diplomatic pouch, hot off the press. I was in Caracas, getting ready to go to Madrid for the launch of the book, as a guest of the publisher. Tío Ramón arranged a dinner in his home, and as dessert was served, he took me by the hand and led me to his room, saying he had a present for me. On his bed were several copies of *The House of the Spirits*. I was so moved that I burst into tears. I always say I saw the book for the first time in El Corte Inglés, a department store in Madrid, but that isn't true. I saw it first on Tío Ramón's bed. You see why I love my stepfather so much? He has the manners of a prince.

Did they cut your original manuscript much?

Not a word. They must have corrected the spelling errors.

Have you ever had an original cut?

No, but once my editors in Finland asked whether they could cut fifteen percent of the book because it was very long in their language. Fifteen percent of what? Each sentence? Each page? A novel isn't like a sausage. Carmen reads my manuscripts, gives me her comments, then they go to the editor and are published. No one, except my mother, corrects my books.

Every time I go on a trip, I find new editions of each of your books, especially *The House of the Spirits*. How many different covers can you remember?

I don't know . . . dozens, maybe. There's one for each language, for different collections, for clubs, paperbacks, and so on. I've tried to keep a collection of first editions, but I'm missing many of them. In some countries they publish my books and don't even have the courtesy to send a copy. And there are others where they print pirated editions and . . . forget any royalties! It's flattering, in a way, but from a financial point of view, I can't say I like it.

I learned that in Chile, an underground press was set up to pirate *Paula*. The book was sold in the streets, on buses, in the theater, like roasted peanuts. When did it really strike home, and how did the reality set in, that you were being read in Europe, in the United States, in Latin America, throughout the entire world?

It happened gradually. . . . It's still hard for me to imagine how far my books have reached. It's a miracle.

When I reread *The House of the Spirits*, which I do each time I teach the book in my literature class, I always have the suspicion that the four female protagonists are four different facets of the same woman: you.

That's an interesting theory. They're not different facets of me, but they could be facets of one character, a very complex woman motivated by love. Nívea, Clara, Blanca, and Alba share character traits: they don't fit in, they rebel against masculine authority, they question their society, and they are romantics with a sense of family and honor.

All four are creative: Clara writes in her notebooks, Blanca makes her crèches. Alba paints an infinite mural; even Rosa the Beautiful embroiders a tablecloth that is never finished. Isn't this a facet of your own personality?

They say that novelists write only about themselves, but themselves in different masks. We are an incorrigibly vain breed.

A Chosen Destiny

You are a bonfire
of stupor as
your thirst blazes.

Pablo Neruda

From the time she was a little girl, she dreamed of heroic deeds, helping the destitute, founding a home for orphans, righting wrongs. She would plug a hole in the dike with her finger and save another Dutch village, she wrote in *Paula*, referring to the legend of Hans in the town of Harlem, Holland. Filled with adventure books read on the sly, she nourished the secret illusion of being a Tom Sawyer, a Black Pirate, or a Sandokán. After she read Shakespeare, she incorporated tragedy into her repertoire, because she wanted to be "one of those magnificent characters that, after living life to the full, dies in the last act." Through her travels and wanderings, her interior kingdom of fantasy grew large. Her television program and her column in *Paula* brought her recognition and popularity, particularly among the youthful sector of the population, which identified with her liberal ideas. Nevertheless, she did not consider that her work in Chile as a journalist was exceptional. Exile in Venezuela, following the military coup of 1973, was a severe blow. There she found herself stripped of everything she had been. "The loneliness that had plagued me since childhood became even more acute, but I consoled myself with the vague hope that I was cut out for a special destiny that someday would be revealed to me."

51

To realize that destiny, she would have to scuttle her ship more than once, and lose some of the crew that had set sail with her. To fulfill her chosen destiny, like the classic hero of Greek tragedy, Isabel would have to know misfortune, fall defeated more than once, and pull herself up again before she reached Ithaca.

On September 11, 1973, when Isabel was thirty-one, the loving wife of Miguel Frías, the happy mother of Paula and Nicolás, her personal life took an unforeseen turn. Until that time, her life had been hectic but filled with rewards. She had come to believe that nothing bad could happen to her family if they did nothing bad. It was all a question of following the rules of the game. Following the military coup, Isabel became piercingly aware of the fate of her fellows. Persecution, torture, summary execution, murder, hunger, terror, impotent rage, unfathomable pain, turned the lives of most Chileans upside down. Isabel felt that "the demons had escaped from the mirrors and were running loose through the world."

Loudly proclaiming her presence in her gaily painted Citroën, Isabel moved through streets patrolled night and day by soldiers with weapons at the ready. The same woman who had collected sick dogs and helped priests in the slums, now helped victims of the dictatorship hide, find asylum in embassies, or slip out of the country. After she received threats, and lost her jobs at *Paula*, at the children's magazine *Mampato*, of which she had been the editor, and on television, she realized that having the name Allende was dangerous, even though her underground activities had not been discovered. And above all, this rebellious woman, who characteristically defied all forms of authority, did not want to, *could not*, live in a dictatorship.

She left Chile in 1975, went to Venezuela, and would not return to her homeland until thirteen years later at the time of a plebiscite. In 1973, she had said: "I did not again think in terms of destiny until the military coup brought me to a brutal confrontation with reality and forced me to take a new direction."

In 1975, the president of Venezuela was Carlos Andrés Pérez. During his term, Venezuela was still riding the crest of the oil bonanza. I was in Caracas in January 1976, and I remember the number of public celebrations and social gatherings. On one occasion, I attended a party where we were served the famous Venezuelan drink *palos*, accompanied by exquisite hors d'oeuvres called *pasapalos*. I noticed with amazement that as soon as I had taken one sip from a glass of the best imported whisky, the waiter would immediately replace it with another, filled to the rim. At the time, that country had the highest per-capita consumption of whisky and champagne in the world.

Venezuela had generously opened its doors to refugees from the Southern Cone. Military dictatorships ruled in Chile, Argentina, and Uruguay, and most of the exiled politicians were middle-class professionals well equipped to contribute to the flourishing Venezuelan economic boom. But so many refugees and immigrants arrived from those countries that they aroused jealousy and suspicion. They were contemptuously called "parcels from Chile," and "those guys from the Southern Cone," and there was great animosity against them among people who felt that the foreigners had displaced them.

Venezuelans are very different from Chileans. "The men strutting with power and virility wore ostentatious chains and rings, joked and spoke at a shout, and always had one eye on the women. Beside them, discreet Chileans with their high-pitched voices and delicate Spanish seemed like dolls on a wedding cake."

Being incorporated into a new society, even into a culture similar to one's own, has a price. Latin America does not have the mobility or penetrability of the United States when it comes to accepting foreigners. For Isabel, the initial years in Caracas were years of paralysis, thus fulfilling one of the prophecies of an Argentine seer who, in 1972, predicted that Salvador Allende would fall in a bloodbath before the year was out; that one of Isabel's children, Paula, would become known around the world; and that after years of immobility, Isabel would become prominent in theater or literature. "From the moment I crossed the cordillera that marks the boundary of Chile, everything began to go badly, and got progressively worse as the years went by."

Although she had never known affluence, neither had Isabel known hard times. In Chile she was someone; in Venezuela she was

unknown. She attempted to get a job as a journalist, with little success. She wrote scripts for television and theater, for which she was
infrequently and minimally compensated. When one of her works
did appear on the screen, she usually was not paid, and when she was
commissioned to write something, she was sometimes paid, but her
work was not performed. She applied for jobs every day, and since
in Venezuela it is considered terribly discourteous to say no, she was
amiably invited to "come back tomorrow." Only after several heart-
breaking frustrations did she learn the social norms of the Caribbean,
so different from those in Chile, where one's word is irrevocable.
Her husband, Miguel, found work at the construction site of a dam
in the interior. Sometimes they were separated for weeks, even
months. Accustomed to a two-income family in Chile, they found
themselves forced to scrimp on expenses in order to be able to send
the children to school. Isabel had lost her financial independence,
and, as she knows so well, there is no women's lib without financial
independence.

She managed to publish a few articles in the Sunday supplement
of the daily *El Nacional*, and its director, Julio Lanzarotti, warned
her that the more sarcastic and cutting Chilean sense of humor
wouldn't go over in Venezuela. She had to learn to look at things in
a different way. "Love of revelry, the sense of living in the present,
and the optimistic vision of the Venezuelans that at first terrified me,
later became the most valued lessons from that time."

Her salvation would come from within, as she turned to the powers of memory and fantasy. In her years as a journalist in Chile, she
was known as a person gifted with a fertile imagination and unlimited exaggeration. After a luncheon of conger eel and white wine
with Pablo Neruda in Isla Negra in the middle of 1973, the poet
refused to be interviewed by Isabel Allende. "My dear child, you
must be the worst journalist in the country. You are incapable of
being objective. You place yourself at the center of everything you
do. I suspect you're not beyond fibbing, and when you don't have
news, you invent it. Why don't you write novels instead? In literature, those defects are virtues."

Delia Vergara, the publisher of *Paula*, was another person who never trusted the authenticity of Isabel's interviews. "She accused me of making up my interviews without ever leaving the house, and of putting my own opinions in the mouths of my subjects, and so she rarely gave me important assignments."

In California, Isabel's grandson Alejandro discovered that his grandmother Mai changed the official line to offer her original versions of classic tales and traditional legends. Alejandro's great-grandfather, Tata, had observed Isabel's ease in telling things in her own style. "I can't trust you, though, because you change everything around. When I die, there won't be anyone to rein you in, and sure as you're born, you'll go around telling lies about me," Tata said.

After suffering a stroke, Tata, through strength of will and pure stubbornness, regained the use of the left side of his body and lived twenty more years, reading the Bible and the Encyclopedia Britannica as he slowly sipped large glasses of water that turned out to be gin, "medicine" that Isabel procured for him when she saw that the treatment was effective. Tata was nearly one hundred years old when he died in Chile; Isabel was then in Caracas, halfway through the letter she had begun writing on January 8, 1981. That grandfather is the character who occupies the most memorable place in Isabel's life. Just as Esteban Trueba outlives all the characters of the first epoch of the book except Tránsito Soto, don Agustín Llona Cuevas was still alive when almost no one of his generation was left in Santiago.

Before she was married, Isabel lived in La Reina, a neighborhood in the foothills of the cordillera, with her mother and her Tío Ramón. During that period, she acquired the custom of stopping by to visit Tata every evening after she left the office. Even after she was married, she went by every afternoon to see her grandfather before she picked up her children at Granny's house. Later she would recall this fertile period of her life. "My daily visits with Tata provided me with enough material for all the books I have written, and possibly all I will write. He was a virtuoso storyteller, gifted with perfidious humor, able to recount the most hair-raising stories while bellowing with laughter. He held back none of the anecdotes accumulated through his many years of living: the principal historical events of the century, the excesses of our family, and the infinite knowledge acquired in his reading. The only forbidden subjects were religion and illness. He considered that God is not a topic for discussion, and that everything connected with the body and its functions is private—to him, even looking in the mirror was a ridiculous vanity, and he shaved by memory."

During that period, Isabel was editor of *Mampato,* a magazine for children, which dovetailed with her work as an editor on *Paula* and with her television program. She was also writing children's stories and plays. In addition to a play entitled *El embajador,* two supper-club extravaganzas she had scripted in the early seventies brought laughter to many people in Chile. Cecilia Viel, a friend from childhood, remembers that on opening night they took Isabel's grandfather, very elderly by that time, and seated him in the front row. The old man was so moved, Cecilia said, that he cried all the way through the performance, and, as she told me about it, even though it had happened more than twenty-five years before, Cecilia herself began to cry and I had to join in. That profound love between grandfather and granddaughter explains the long letter Isabel began to write him from Caracas, which ended as the manuscript of her first novel.

Without knowing it, she had been writing *The House of the Spirits* in her mind. It took the disruption of exile and disillusion of love, as well as the news that her grandfather was dying and inexorably taking with him Isabel's youth, to light the flame. Within her was the entire story to be told, the voices of the spirits waiting to be convoked. She gave them a day and a date on which to begin to speak: January 8, 1981.

Of Love and Shadows

The year 1973 appears in your work with some frequency, and it swells in a kind of crescendo through all your writing until the coup d'etat, which affected your life personally. But to go further back in time, what do you remember of the early elections in Chile, when you were in grade school?

I remember the one in which Carlos Ibáñez del Campo, a cavalry officer, was elected. Before that, he had been a kind of dictator, and people feared him; it was said that while he was governing, many people were tortured and murdered, and bodies were thrown into the ocean with rocks tied to their ankles. In my house they spoke of this man as if he were a demon. On election day I was so afraid I threw up; I thought he was going to kill us all, and I was almost disappointed when nothing happened. Compared with what the military did later, Ibáñez was a Santa Teresa. That was the first time I was aware that people voted, that there was a political process.

Was Ibáñez's a military government?

No, civil. The second time he stood as a candidate, and was elected.

He was a friend of Perón. In Argentina, he was called *caballo Ibáñez*. Do you think that Chilean politics affected your personal situation and your vocation as a writer?

That came much later, with the military coup of 1973.

You made a huge leap when *The House of the Spirits* **was published in Spain.**

I wrote that book in 1981. You were asking me about the social theme that is repeated so often in my books. In 1981, most Latin American writers were living in forced exile, or had left their countries because they couldn't live under the crushing dictatorships. That was a fatal decade in Latin America; half the population of the continent was living under a dictatorship. The literature of that period is marked by exile. I wasn't the only one preoccupied with social and political themes.

Where and how did you begin to develop the theme of *Of Love and Shadows?*

When my agent, Carmen Balcells, accepted the manuscript of *The House of the Spirits*, she told me that anyone can write a good first book, but that talent is proved with the second. I took her words very seriously. I wanted to know whether or not I was a writer, and I threw myself into a second novel, still writing at night because I couldn't give up my job. I didn't have to choose the theme. In 1978 a political crime was uncovered in Chile: the corpses of fifteen campesinos who had been massacred by the military in 1973. Their bodies had been buried in the abandoned lime kilns near Lonquén. The Catholic church revealed the truth before the military authorities could cover it up. I was in Venezuela when I heard that news published around the world, and without knowing why, I cut the article out of the newspaper. That was long before I began writing; literature wasn't in my mind then.

Then why did you collect those clippings?

I think maybe the ghosts of those murdered campesinos refused to leave me in peace until I wrote their story. I also had tapes of people who had been tortured in Chile. Shortly after the coup, a person came to my office who was on the staff of the magazine. He had disappeared for several months, and when he returned, he was a different person. He showed me the scars of his torture, told me his experience, and agreed to let me tape his story. From that moment, I began to keep a record of the oppression, as several other journalists were doing; it was a duty to do that, even though we couldn't use the material because the censorship was too ferocious. Some of that information was later published in Europe, especially in Germany. I had had those tapes for years without listening to them. In Venezuela I also had the opportunity to interview exiles who had been in Chilean concentration camps. In 1975, in Caracas, I interviewed Dr. Arturo Jirón, Salvador Allende's physician, who had been in La Moneda on the day of the coup. He told me what he had experienced inside the burning palace that last day: Allende's death, his own arrest, torture, and banishment to Dawson Island, where he was held prisoner, and then his exile. That was my source for Jaime's torture scene in *The House of the Spirits*. I interviewed several others, among them the highest-ranking Chilean official in exile, a man who refused to carry out an order to shoot others and was expelled from the country, and was then selling insurance in Caracas. He was the inspiration and model for the character of Gustavo Morante in *Of Love and Shadows*. I was able to use that information when I wrote the novel in 1983. I listened to the tapes again, reread the press clippings, and called on my memory.

Those were true events; however, in the novel you carefully avoided mentioning the place and date those crimes took place. Why? Were you afraid that the long arm of the Chilean dictatorship would reach you in Venezuela, as it did Orlando Letelier in Washington?

No, that thought never occurred to me. I did it for the same reason I never mentioned Chile in *The House of the Spirits*, a book that could not be more Chilean. By not specifying time and place, more people could identify with the story. Those crimes could have occurred in Greece during the era of the colonels, in Central Europe, in Argentina and Uruguay during the dirty war, in any country of Central America.

All Latin America was politically unstable; there were dictatorships everywhere, brutal repression. Political exiles could have formed a nation the size of Norway, García Márquez said in his Nobel acceptance speech. Unfortunately, the exiles were scattered across the world.

The military committed terrible atrocities in Argentina, Chile, and Uruguay. *Of Love and Shadows* also recounts my experience as a journalist in the times of terror. What I wrote about Irene is almost identical to the atmosphere I lived in: apparent normality, but, within that, somber reality. Just as I did in real life, in the novel Irene taped interviews with the agents of repression, and with their victims. Like me, she was not able to publish that material; she hid the tapes with the idea of salvaging truth from oblivion. She also found herself involved in covert activities. Describing all that was easy because I had lived it.

In the mythic space you created for the novel, you were very faithful to actual geography. I know a student who, for his thesis, went to Chile to research the flora and fauna of the setting; it coincides exactly with what you described in the novel. That is ant-like intensity.

To make a work believable, it's important to verify such details. In this case, it was a matter of remembering, but for the town of Agua Santa in *Eva Luna* and *The Stories of Eva Luna*, another "mythic space" as you call it, I had to do careful research. I couldn't have peaches in Agua Santa, just as I couldn't have mangos in Los Riscos.

Almost the same thing happened with your second novel that happened with *The House of the Spirits:* first, success in Europe, much later in Latin America, and finally, in the United States. Why do you think the international reaction to your work was so uniform?

I don't know. I suppose that *The House of the Spirits* paved the way for the books that followed. Soon, Latin American editors became interested, and negotiations have become easier with each book. Also, readers who enjoyed the first novel have kept buying the later ones. I have a very faithful public. When I do a signing, people often come with all my books in a tote, as if they collected them. In the United States they say I'm a "long-seller."

What do you think about the movie based on that book?

I liked it a lot; it's faithful to the text and to the Chilean reality of the time. I think that it's one of Antonio Banderas's best roles. It's difficult for me to watch that film with any objectivity. I always start crying halfway through, and toward the end, I'm sobbing because the actress Jennifer Connelly looks so much like Paula. The resemblance is so surprising that the first time I saw her in person I thought she was a ghost, and felt weak in the knees. In the film there is a long scene in the hospital in which she is connected to a respirator, exactly the image I have of my daughter in the hospital in Madrid.

Of Love and Shadows **can be classified as a political novel. In any case, it's the most political of all your works. José Martí wrote: "I want to cast my fate/ with the poor of the earth/ the rushing mountain stream/ lulls me more than the sea." This solidarity with the poor made me think of your support of Survivors International, to whom you donated the proceeds of the movie premiere of** *De amor y de sombra* **in San Francisco. You also donated those from** *The House of the Spirits* **to the AIDS Foundation. You established fellowships in Paula's name at San Jose State. You help wherever you can, even in Bangladesh, and now you have created an Isabel Allende Foundation for education. What has driven you to help "the poor of the earth," those poor in more than one sense?**

A restless heart and the certainty that I have been given a lot and that I must go naked to the grave. One possesses only what one gives away. That, my daughter Paula taught me with her joyful openhandedness, and with the terrible lesson of her suffering and her death.

**In an interview conducted by Eleanor Wachtel, you said that you
are neutral in matters of politics. Do you also realize that prob-
ably the one socialist to be found in a middle-class neighborhood
during the military coup of 1973 was you? Although you did not
belong to the party, you voted for Allende, and afterward you
opposed the dictatorship. What official position do you hold currently in regard to oppressive governments in Latin America?**

First of all, I don't remember ever having said I am neutral, only
that I did not, and do not, actively participate in political parties. I
mistrust all of them. My position is always to defend the least
favored; people with that view used to be called leftists, and here in
the United States, they're scornfully labeled liberals. This is the only
country I know where being called a liberal or a virgin is an insult.
As for oppressive governments in Latin America or anywhere else in
the world, I will always oppose them.

Eva Luna

Each of your works corresponds to a stage of your life. The first two novels have to do with the trauma of the military coup in Chile, and your exile. I see feminism as the theme of *Eva Luna*. The protagonist speaks for you; she is a living exponent of your feminist ideals.

There are two basic themes in that book: feminism and narration. This is something I am able to tell you now, after reading the criticism and several doctoral theses on the book, but when I write, I have no idea what I'm doing. I had written two novels and finally I felt I was a full-fledged writer. For the first time, as I was completing a form in the airport, I dared put the magic word "writer" in the space indicating *profession*. All my life I had flirted around the edge of literature—journalism, children's stories, television scripts, humor, two novels translated into a number of languages, and millions of letters—but I still didn't feel like a writer. Using that word was a major step; it was assuming my destiny and living it fully.

In *Eva Luna*, readers do not know whether you are writing about the real life of the protagonist, the novelized life she invents for herself, or the television series she's writing.

The story moves on three levels, and relates everything Eva Luna feels when she discovers she can write the wealth of stories she carries within her. The book is dotted with autobiographical observations about the practice of writing. Where inspiration comes from, how writing transforms one's life, how a banal existence can be converted into the subject of a novel—all those things are found in *Eva Luna*.

What was happening in your life as you were writing your third novel?

In Venezuela, my marriage was beginning to unravel, as almost always happens with exiles; the support system that sustains the couple in its own surroundings is stretched thin, and both are left naked. That is the moment of truth. Masks fall, illusions . . . Miguel was working in the interior of Venezuela, in Puerto Ordaz, and I had stayed behind in Caracas with the children, which contributed to our growing apart. I couldn't find work, I couldn't get used to where I was, we didn't have any money, I lived with my face turned to the south, with the idea of going home the moment democracy was restored in Chile. I was depressed, I felt I was a failure; I was thirty years old and hadn't found my destiny; I thought I had done nothing worthwhile, and everything around me seemed flat and mediocre. I was trapped on a dead-end street. Six years later, writing came along to save me. After *The House of the Spirits* and *Of Love and Shadows* were published, I realized that I could earn a living writing fiction. I left the school where I had been working and wrote *Eva Luna* during the daytime, in an office in my house, in my own space, with every comfort, including a computer. But my marriage with Miguel was deteriorating beyond repair. Fortunately, the children were nearly grown and were getting ready to go to college; my role as mother was no longer my only priority.

Had you thought of leaving Venezuela on your own after you published your second book?

No, that came after the third. When I finished *Eva Luna,* I decided to emigrate to Mexico City. There was a string of curious coincidences, which is beside the point here, that allowed me to move my family to that country. We had even picked out a house and were on the verge of buying it with Miguel, despite our problems as a couple, but the day we were to sign the papers, there was so much pollution in the air that birds were falling dead out of the skies. We decided we couldn't live in a city where even the birds can't breathe.

That happens in a story by García Márquez, "One Day After Saturday."

You can see that magical realism is more "real" than "magical" on our continent. They say that if Kafka had been born in Latin America, he would have been tagged a slice-of-life writer. We didn't buy the house, and everything turned out for the best, because shortly after that, Miguel and I made a definite break and I came to the United States.

Using *Eva Luna* as a pretext, let's talk about feminism. You have often said that it has been a determining factor in your character and your life. Have you had macho partners?

No. I've had the good luck to avoid them. Don't forget that my grandfather and my stepfather, the two male pillars of my childhood, were terrifyingly macho. From them, I learned that machos don't change; you have to wait for them to die.

Can you remember the first time you had a feminist awareness, if we can put it that way?

On the gut level, I felt it when I was five, when my mother would tell me "sit with your legs together, like a little lady" and my brothers would be climbing trees in the patio. You realize that by the time I wrote *Eva Luna* that attitude had jelled completely. It had been ripening for nearly forty years. . . .

Your early love for Miguel Frías, or Michael, as you called him, is objectively portrayed in *Paula*. You recognize his merits. You know how to give credit to those who have been good to you; as they say in the fairy tale, "I am going to reward you because you have been kind to me." You do that with your mother-in-law, grandmother to your children, married to a man who washed his hands compulsively. "Granny" to your little ones. Tell me if there was anything in your initial relationship with Miguel that would be important in your future life or your development as a writer.

When I was first married, I had a lot of stored-up anger, anger I couldn't identify: against authority, patriarchy, everything masculine, the Catholic church, my social milieu, my family. That made me rebellious, aggressive. Years later, when I was exposed to socialist theory and the journalists on the magazine *Paula*, I began to read books on feminism and was able to put that hazy indignation of my early youth into words. Miguel was infinitely patient with me. I included him in my generalized rage; often I attacked him or unjustly undervalued him. Miguel was never a macho; he was the last person to deserve my feminist attacks. He gave me space; he kept a prudent distance and let me explore, experiment, change. Perhaps, if he hadn't, I would have taken it by force, but the fact is that I was given room to build a life different from that of most of the women of my generation in Chile, and that later served as underpinning for my writing. I also had two children with Miguel, and that marked me forever. To a degree, I excluded him from my relationship with the children; I took over the children so obsessively that I didn't give him many opportunities to be a father. If I had to define myself, in all fairness I would have to say that more than anything I am an unremitting mother, and that my poor children have had to put up with me. Miguel gave me a long, faithful, and patient affection that enabled me, among many other things, to gain confidence in myself as a woman. On the one hand, I served my husband like a geisha—my friends from those days still make fun of me for it—but, on the other hand, I was very independent and excluded him from essential decisions.

He must have had some defect, too?

None. He was perfect. Everyone said he was a saint . . . for putting up with me, I suppose.

You describe him in *Paula* as being so perfect that some readers—among them, several of my students—have wondered why you stopped loving him. . . . From what "essential decisions" did you exclude him?

Oh, the children, for example. I took them over completely. Even choices in how to run the family were mine alone; he took a passive role. In domestic matters, as well as our social life, I was in charge. And don't forget that it was because of me that we left Chile. None of that was fair to him.

That's an Amazon feminism, very different from what you see in *Eva Luna,* which is a kind of tranquil freedom and self-sufficiency that doesn't need to be aggressive. You're describing a husband who is so passive that he seems not to be there. Why did you choose him?

We chose each other; we fell madly in love. For both of us, it was the first love—because the big-eared kid in Bolivia doesn't count. I loved Miguel very much for many years.

***Eva Luna* marks the end of your marriage. Was it a violent or drastic moment?**

Painful, because nearly always divorce is experienced as a loss or a failure, but it wasn't violent or drastic because emotionally we had been separated for years. That relationship had ended long before.

Could we say that your third novel also closes a stage in your life, as if the character had exorcised the demons of youth?

It's true. Starting with that book, I have lived my writing with great assurance, and feminism with the same tranquil freedom you say you see in *Eva Luna.* I don't go around anymore kicking doors or insulting machos; I realize that it's futile, although I haven't lost the ideals I had when I was young. The form has changed, not the content.

Do you think you chose a passive husband out of resentment for your absent father, someone you really never knew? (*She gives me a cautious look.*)

No, because in that case I would have used the same criteria to choose a second, and Willie could not be a more present and active partner. My father's absence was so total, so drastic and dramatic, it was as if an arm or a leg had been amputated. I couldn't feel resentment or nostalgia for someone who might as well have been a total stranger.

When an extremity is amputated, it hurts. All the women in your work have absent or unreachable fathers: Blanca Trueba, Irene Beltrán, Eva Luna, Belisa Crepusculario, and so on.

Their fathers aren't there, but occasionally, there is a substitute, like Riad Halabí in *Eva Luna*.

With the exception of Esteban Trueba and Gregory Reeves, women are your strongest characters, even in the case of the Ranquileos in *Of Love and Shadows;* Digna is the mainstay of that family, while the father, Eusebio, goes off with the circus. Of all your female characters, would you say that Eva Luna is the strongest?

I don't remember all my female characters, but I did put in Eva Luna's mouth everything I always wanted to say about the female condition; undoubtedly, she is very strong. But I think that hers is a practical feminism, assumed very naturally. In my case, for many years I suffered what my mother calls reverse machismo.

Wrong or right, it gave you a special push.

I could do it because I was earning a living and didn't have to ask anyone for money. I started working very early, and I kept on working after I married. That gave me freedom. That's also the key to Eva Luna's freedom; she learns at an early age to earn her living.

Do you think that feminism has run its course? There is a lot of talk about the revisionism that has cut off, or reversed, the movement of women's liberation.

Feminism is a revolution on the march; it has highs and lows, but it can't be turned back now. And it hasn't really achieved much; the great majority of humanity has never heard of equal rights for women. They are still being sold like cattle, beaten to death, scarred, mutilated. Violence against women is called "domestic" violence, as if it were somehow less violent for being directed against women—

and no one cares very much. In India I saw highways being built by hand. The men are considered laborers; women are their "helpers," and although they do the same work, they earn half what the men do. Dressed in their colorful saris, with their children riding their hips or strapped to their backs, they carry cement and iron on their heads, their picks level hills, and they transport mountains stone by stone in their baskets. From afar they are elegant apparitions, mirages of the roadway, but when you see them up close you see the brutal wasting, the effect of bad nutrition, the marks of pregnancies and hard labor. By twenty, they are ancient; they live a much shorter time than the men and their lives are pure struggle and pain. At night, these exhausted women cook the meals, tend the children, serve their husbands, haul water, wash the clothes, and, before they go to sleep, they eat what is left from others' plates and then by the light of a candle embroider beautiful cushions, blouses, belts, and tapestries to lend a touch of beauty to their miserable reality. That's why, when I buy any of those things made by a woman's hand, I feel a mixture of reverence and sadness for every stitch.

When it is a woman's creation, it is called a "craft" and is not highly valued, but when it is something made by a man, it's called "art," and is much more highly regarded.

Exactly, just as men's beliefs are called religions and women's are classified as superstitions; masculine ideas are philosophy and women's are emotional outpourings. The most frequent domestic accident in India is the one suffered by young wives who die of fatal burns. Gasoline "falls" on them and they go up like living torches, watched by the husband and the mother-in-law who are then free to obtain another wife and another dowry. It's more expeditious than divorce, and apparently, the police never relate these numerous "accidents" with how fast the widowers remarry. In Muslim countries, the situation is even worse. When a man prays to Allah, he begins by giving thanks that he was not born a woman. There's a good reason for that; in most places in the world, a poor woman's worth is less than the price of a lamb. Feminism is a comparatively new idea, but I feel sure that, like fire fanned by the wind, it will inexorably spread. I won't live to see the results, but maybe my granddaughters will. That gives me happiness in this long struggle.

In *Eva Luna* there is another important theme: *mestizaje,* mixed blood.

Which is also a part of my life and my character, Celia. When I wrote that novel, I was living in the midst of *mestizaje.* I was very aware of races, of the two cultures I saw around me: that of the south of the continent and that of the Caribbean. I realized that I am the daughter of all the migrations that crept across the hallucinatory geography of our continent, all their traditions, languages, beliefs, unbridled greed, hatreds and loves, all blended together in a crucible of violence, lust, and, yes, love. The Latin American peoples are the result of all those things, which doesn't mean that we're a homogeneous culture. There are enormous differences between the peoples of the Southern Cone and those of the Caribbean, between those from the mountains and those on the coast. *Mestizaje* is an inexhaustible source of richness in literature and the arts. The boom of Latin American literature is a chorus of different, but harmonious voices that have communicated our fabulous continent to the world and given us a sense of identity and an inarguable *mestizo* identity. Blacks, Indians, whites, all singing. I wrote that book with such gusto! It was a fiesta of senses and ideas.

***Eva Luna* has less of your own personal history than previous books, and yet Eva is your favorite female character, the one you most identify with. Why?**

Because she rebels against her destiny and makes her way by using the one gift nature gave her: the gift of telling a story. Because she is feminine and feminist. Because she has a just heart, and does not fear her sensuality.

Are you like that?

I aspire to be like that.

The Stories of Eva Luna

Your stories move really fast. You can read them in one burst, and then read them a second time with the same newness as the first; they're magical books. The fast-moving pace you developed in journalism gave you the dexterity to be at ease in short fiction. How did you become a short-story writer?

Out of pure necessity. When I came to California, I moved in with Willie, at 5 Marina Way in San Rafael. It was a small, chaotic place, besides being crowded with strange beings. There was no physical place where I could hide, much less write, and so I set up a table practically on top of Willie's bed, where I wrote by hand in lined notebooks while chaos reigned on the other side of the door: Willie's children fighting, the dog barking, and the television thundering. Sometimes I escaped with Willie to his office and sat in a corner to scribble in my notebook. I had reverted to the times of my first novel, when I wrote in the kitchen at night or at stolen moments during the day—with the difference that in California I didn't have the emotional tranquility I had in 1981 when I began *The House of the Spirits*. I was living in a whirlwind of passions. You can understand that it is impossible to write a novel that way. The great advantage of short stories is that they can be completed in a reasonable period of time; everything else about them is difficult.

How long did it take you to write the twenty-three pieces in *The Stories of Eva Luna?*

A year, but I wrote others that weren't included. That was a crazy year; I was discovering love with Willie, but I still had all my roots in Venezuela, where I had lived for thirteen years, and my children, my house, everything I owned, were waiting for me. In addition, I had a contract to teach one semester at the University of Virginia. I spent six months flying back and forth across the continent. Willie and I would travel all day to be together just one night, then climb back on a plane the next day.

Would you do that today?

Today I wouldn't teach the semester at Virginia. (*She laughs with that contagious laugh that makes her audiences join in wherever they hear her.*)

The stories are very different, but their principal setting is tropical—although sometimes Chile appears without being identified. Why are nearly all set in Venezuela?

Because they're being told by Eva Luna. They are all love stories; that's the thread that ties them together. And it isn't strange they should share the same theme, because at the age of forty-five, I had fallen in love like a schoolgirl.

However, you said in one of the stories, "Our Secret," that fear is stronger than love.

If I had to write that story again, I would say that love is much stronger than fear. I believe that nothing is as strong as love; it's stronger than hatred, rage . . . anything.

Do you believe in the all-embracing power of love to rescue a person from any previous condition?

I do. (*She says this emphatically.*)

What was the inspiration for "The Judge's Wife"?

Which one is that? I don't remember.

It's about an elderly judge who's married to a young woman. There is an outlaw the judge decides to bring to justice by using the bandit's mother as bait. He locks the poor woman in a cage in the center of the plaza and leaves her there without water, with the hope that her moans will attract her son. But everything gets turned around, and at the end there is a confrontation between the outlaw, who is intent on revenge, and the judge's young wife. He falls in love with her. . . . The man loses his head for a few hours of love.

Ah, the foolishness one writes! I think that story was born of an image from a black-and-white Western: a woman stepping down from a stagecoach in a dusty street; an elderly man in a frock coat is helping her, and on the roof of some nearby buildings you see the heads of a group of men—apparent bandits—who have the two in their sights. That image stayed with me until I was able to exorcise it. The whole story derived from that persistent image; one thing was linked to another, and then another, almost without conscious thought, as nearly always happens when I write. The level of tragedy kept going up, and I ended with a strange and unplanned denouement.

But you've said that before you write the first line of a story, you have to have the whole thing in your head.

That's true—the story appears like an apple, whole. But sometimes it comes wrapped up, and you have to tear the wrapping away. When I say I came to an unplanned denouement, I mean that I wanted a happy ending, but the story was "written," and I had no choice but to put it down just as it was.

Your life is highly powered by the force of love. Sometimes even when dealing with people you don't know, you do it with affection, and you don't have a prejudiced bone in your body. You've traveled, you've seen a lot of the world, and you've recognized that human beings are the same everywhere. You accept personal, cultural, racial differences with great naturalness. In all your books, in one way or other, you introduce good and evil. Evil is repre-

sented by corrupt systems; you propose that power corrupts.

It seems I've had more sympathy for the underworld than for authority.

Your best characters are marginalized. You move along, winning over your reader, ensnaring him in your story, in love and suspense, so he will feel the same sympathy for the downtrodden that you feel. And the reader waits for a monumental force to appear to protect the helpless, the orphaned, the uprooted. The reader wants with all his heart for that protagonist to be saved, for him to come out the winner, for him not to be defeated by the machinery of the corrupt system. And, sooner or later, your characters who have known power suffer disillusionment. When they are sufficiently honest, like Esteban Trueba, they are finally transformed; if not, they are defeated. When liberty is snuffed out in his country, Esteban loses his power and his granddaughter is tortured; he sinks into the depths of pain. Even so, there is no didactic or moralistic flavor to your work. Your stories take unexpected directions; the ends can't be foreseen.

Esteban Trueba lives long enough to see the consequences of his acts. Very few of us are able to do that. If we knew that each act, each thought, each intention produces a series of consequences, we would be much more cautious in life.

You're right. And the descendants whom we'll never know, as if in a chain reaction, will suffer from actions we take today. The human condition does not include seeing into the future.

As you know, for years I went by to have a cup of tea with my grandfather every day. You can't imagine how much I learned from him. He was born with a defective hip joint, which got worse with age, but he was very athletic and never accepted his physical limitations. An electric wheelchair would have eased his last years, but he was so proud that no one in the family dared suggest it. His physical condition forced him to spend a lot of time meditating on the past. He used to tell me that good memory is a curse, because you remember all your errors, and all their consequences. Those months I spent at Paula's bedside were like the years of my grandfather's old age: a time of immobility and meditation. In those months, I was able to see clearly paths I had traveled blindly.

Your memory is accurate in the stories, as is your erotic tone. And several of your stories are notable for their irony. "Toad's Mouth," however, is written with overt and slightly vulgar humor that must have provoked more than one moralistic objection.

Some readers were horrified by "Toad's Mouth." The story is banned in Mormon schools, and heads the blacklist of many Christian fundamentalist and other groups. My mother opposed it so strongly that I nearly pulled it from the book.

It amused me because we played "toad" in our house, but not the game your protagonist Hermelinda excelled at; ours was much more innocent. That story reminds me of the sometimes brazen humor of Boccaccio. What was its origin?

There is a legend in Chile about a woman like the protagonist of the story, who earned her living in Patagonia by opening her legs so men could throw coins aimed at her most private parts. They say she founded a dynasty, one of the most powerful families of the territory, owners of large landholdings claimed from the Indians with bullets, extortion, and alcohol.

Was that woman's name Hermelinda?

No, I gave her that name in my story; why would I use the real woman's name? She died years ago, although in Chile there are still people who recognized her in my fictional character. My mother says that the book struck her descendants like a slap in the face.

Did a man really come along and take her away, along with the

money she'd earned playing "toad's mouth"?

No, I invented that part. I like happy endings.

I suspect that several of these stories were taken from real life.

Oh, they were. Some came directly from articles in newspapers.

"And Of Clay Are We Created" is based on a catastrophe that occurred in Colombia when a volcano erupted, isn't it?

In 1985 the Nevado Ruiz volcano became active; the snow at the peak melted, and that caused an avalanche of mud and rock that buried a village below. So many people died that they couldn't recover the bodies, so they declared the entire zone a cemetery. A girl, Omayra Sánchez, died there buried in mud up to her armpits in the rubble of her house and the bodies of her family. It took her three whole days to die. The world press filmed her dying face. I saw it on Caracas television. Her big black eyes, filled with resignation and wisdom, still pursue me in dreams. Writing the story failed to exorcise her ghost.

But the story doesn't really belong to Omayra.

No, it's the story of the man who held her and stayed with her during her long agony, and of the woman watching the man holding the girl, and how that event put both of them in touch with their most profound memories, how it transformed them.

What other stories came from newspapers?

Just a minute. I have to look at the titles because I don't remember the names. (*Checks the table of contents.*) "Interminable Life" is based on the story of a pair of elderly immigrants in Venezuela who committed suicide together. He was a very well-known scientist. The idea of "The Road North" came to me when the Catholic church in Honduras denounced the kidnapping of poor children being killed in order to sell their vital organs in wealthy countries. When that story was published, many people thought it was a product of my morbid imagination, because they couldn't believe that anything like that could occur in the real world. Today, it's a known fact that this revolting traffic isn't limited to Honduras. . . . The story of "A Discreet Miracle" happened in Chile to a friend of mine who's a priest, and I told it faithfully, without changing his name. "If You Touched My Heart" I took from another newspaper article in Venezuela: the case of a woman whom a jealous husband locked up in a cellar for fifty years. When she was rescued, they found a blind monster covered with scales and with nails long as claws, who had forgotten human language.

In your stories, you create atmosphere with a pencil stroke. In several you use the town of Agua Santa, which also appears in *Eva Luna*. You also create a mythic space in Tres Marías, the hacienda in *La casa de los espíritus*.

Those places must exist somewhere, Celia, because it seems to me that I didn't invent them—they rose up like a trick of memory, each with its smells, its temperature, its landscape. Agua Santa and Las Tres Marías got me out of many holes.

What differences do you find between the technique of the novel and that of the short story?

I have sometimes said that the novel is like embroidering a tapestry with many threads and colors; it's a sum of details, all a question of patience. I embroider blindly, but one day I turn over the tapestry and see the design on the right side. With a little luck, in the spell of the whole, the defects are unseen. A short story, on the other hand, is like shooting an arrow—you have only one chance. The hand and keen eye of a good archer are required to control direction, force, and velocity. How many thousands of short stories have you read, and how many can you remember? Yet, however bad a novel may be, you can always say what it was about. The novel unfolds gradually, almost on its own, revealing its mysteries to you. In a story, if you are to create adequate tension and tone, you must know everything that is to happen before you write the first line. It must be read in a single breath; if the reader interrupts the momentum, leaves the story, it won't work. Short fiction is closer to poetry than to the novel. There's no time or space; nothing can be added or taken away; every defect is visible. The novel is written with a solid plot, defined characters, and patience. The story is a question of tone. It is written with inspiration and no little luck.

The Infinite Plan

Which of your male characters do you like best? Remember that Flaubert said, *"Madame Bovary, c'est moi!"*

Gregory Reeves, in *The Infinite Plan*. I like him so much that in real life, I married him some years ago, and not even marriage has made me stop liking him.

***The Infinite Plan* is based on the life of your husband, William Gordon. How much is fiction and how much reality?**

I don't honestly know. I think all my books, with the exception of *Eva Luna* and a few stories, are much more reality than fiction. In *The Infinite Plan*, the characters are based on human models, and nearly everything that happens is real. Sometimes I needed two people to create a character, as was the case with Carmen/Tamar. The models were Carmen Álvarez, a childhood friend of Willie's, and Tabra Tunoa, my good friend, who gave me her biography to use for Tamar. Gregory Reeves was very easy, since Willie was the model. As with Clara del Valle, in *The House of the Spirits*, I didn't have to invent the character; it was there, waiting for me. No need to exhaust my imagination.

All those things couldn't have happened in Willie's life!

That's what a critic said in a San Francisco newspaper—that it was unrealistic that so many things could have occurred in one lifetime. The truth was that actually I had to leave parts out because the real story seemed exaggerated. I didn't mention, for example, that Willie had a delinquent son; the tragedy of his poor, drug-addicted daughter was enough. Nor did I tell the story of his adopted son, which is more than enough for another book. I skipped many violent anecdotes about his father, as well as the fact that his mother tried to rid herself of Willie by putting him in orphanages or giving him up for adoption.

That part you do tell.

Not as it truly happened, which was much worse than what I wrote in the book. The one part that I expanded, instead of cut, was the chapter about Vietnam. Willie was in the army, but not on the battlefield as described in the book. An ex-Vietnam vet told me that part.

What was Willie's reaction when he read the book? Weren't you afraid he would be horrified to find himself exposed in those pages, with all his problems and faults?

My mother said it would lead to a divorce, but none of it was a surprise to him because we had discussed each chapter. When I met him and he began to tell me the story of his life, I knew I had to write it, and I think that was why I fell so quickly and so deeply in love. From the very beginning, I told him what I had in mind; there was nothing hidden. I spent four years sleeping with that story, checking details, asking questions, visiting the places where events had occurred, interviewing dozens of people. When he read the book, Willie told me, deeply moved, "This is a map of my life; now I understand where I've been." The danger with that, of course, is that now he thinks he's Gregory Reeves and goes around worrying about who will play him in the film. He thinks Paul Newman is a little short. . . .

Don't you sometimes feel that Gregory Reeves is more real than Willie? Or is it the reverse?

Who can know? Maybe I invent everything. Even people.

What do you mean?

I ask myself if Willie exists or if I invented Gregory Reeves in *The Infinite Plan* and dressed Willie in his clothing. Which one lives with me, the real Willie or the literary one? And my mother? Because I have talked about her so much, have I invented the mother I like and need? Maybe the actual person doesn't fit my descriptions. That idea disturbs and fascinates me. Maybe I attribute qualities and virtues to the people I use for characters that then hang around their necks like a necklace, identities they can't rid themselves of. I invented faults for my grandfather in order to create the character of Esteban Trueba, and he was stuck with them forever, poor man. Much of what I see in Willie may be the superimposed image of Gregory Reeves, but deep down I believe that the character and the person are very much alike. They both are survivors; corks that sink and bob back up again and again; strong, formidable men filled with flaws, passions, and generosity; men who plunge into life with no fear.

Like Miguel de Unamuno, you put yourself into your novels and make them part of your life. Now you are part of the life of Gregory Reeves.

It's a form of madness; I'm sure Freud had a name for it. My destiny is no more dramatic than anyone else's, but I have found a way to tell it in Technicolor.

What was the reaction to this California-based novel, so different from the others you had published?

Public reaction to *The Infinite Plan* was mixed. Many of my readers were confused because it is about California, and because for the first time I told the story of a man, unlike my earlier books in which the protagonists are women. Critics were divided, but sales were the same as for my other books.

Through Gregory Reeves's eyes, you can appreciate fifty years of

the history and the complex texture of California. You included many races in the novel: whites, Hispanics, blacks, Asians . . . everything. But let's get back to the protagonist and the person who inspired him. Is it true that the first attraction between Willie and you was purely sexual, as I heard you say once in a lecture?

Willie says it was a meeting of souls, but I didn't feel anything spiritual, just pure lust. I had been living a chaste life for a long time . . . two or three weeks, at least! But it wasn't only that—I'd had more exciting relationships; I suppose that on a very basic level we recognized each other. We were two shipwreck victims from distant shores; we had suffered losses and disenchantments, long periods of loneliness. We had as our only capital a hurricane-like energy that had blown us through life, overcoming obstacles; we each recognized in the other that capacity for survival.

Is fidelity important?

There are couples who don't have that rule and who work things out for the best, but since Willie and I know the dangers of including third parties in a relationship, we've made a pact of fidelity. Besides that, I am very jealous, and if I catch him making eyes at some blonde, I'll kill him. Since I don't have time to spy on him, this honor code is best; it saves energy.

But you have not always been faithful . . .

I have with Willie, not only out of virtue, but also lack of opportunity. There aren't that many candidates eager to seduce someone's grandmother. As for the past, I regret the lies and betrayals in my first marriage; they leave indelible scars. Betrayal is always serious.

I asked your husband what your worst fault is, and he told me that you're very domineering. Do you agree?

(*On the defensive*) That's what they say in my family. I want to protect my own and make their lives easy, but I learned something from my daughter's death: I learned that I don't control anything. If I couldn't protect my daughter from death, how can I protect my son or my grandchildren from life? Experience has taught me to be a little hands off with the ones I love.

I don't see you being "hands off" when it comes to your family!

Have all of you been talking about me behind my back? I'm sure they've told you that I stick my nose into everything and have an opinion on every subject. But, in all honesty, I don't know what they're complaining about, especially Willie, because he makes a lot of our decisions, from what we'll have to eat for dinner to where we'll go on vacation or invest our money. He's like a big dog that does a lot of barking; he makes noise and claims his space. He isn't the kind of person who lets himself be dominated.

And what is his worst fault?

I don't know. His greatest virtue is his big heart. This great hunk of a man has the soul of a sweet young girl.

Your house, like your office, even Willie's office, has your individual seal.

Willie has terrible taste; if I'm careless, he ends up in checked pants and buys porcelain dolphins. (*Laughs*) I know, taste is a very personal thing, and what right do I have to criticize Willie? And on and on. I've heard that a thousand times. But we have an agreement: I take care of the house and he oversees the garden; that way, we don't fight. I need order and cleanliness around me; I like to be surrounded with beautiful objects, unique things I buy on trips. The problem is that I'm not really tied to them, so every once in a while—rather often—I give everything away and start over. I like changing paintings and furniture, painting walls and tearing up floors. Willie and Nicolás are terrified of me. When they feel that I'm about to have an attack of redecorating, they flee, because they have to do all the work. I just furnish the ideas.

Do you pry much into the lives of others?

Of course I do. If I didn't pry, I wouldn't have anything to write about. Besides, I know better than anyone else what's best for my family. (*Laughs, openly amused*)

Do you think of yourself as a matriarch? Is it true that you went out to look for a sweetheart for Nicolás after he got divorced?

Well, why wouldn't I? Nicolás was as good as paralyzed; he wasn't going to find another woman if he didn't get moving. That was an idea that came to me after a trip to India. There, ninety-seven percent of marriages are arranged by the parents, and the divorce rate is very low. Besides that, I didn't force Nicolás; I just looked for the perfect woman for him and then introduced them. They fell madly in love at first sight and are very happy, but instead of getting down on their knees to thank me, they tease me and say I stick my nose into everything.

What other faults do you have?

I'm naive. It's easy to deceive me if you come at me from my sentimental side. And I'm very independent; I don't want anyone nosing into my life the way I do in theirs. I rarely ask advice, and when I do, I don't listen. I don't want to be given anything; I detest presents, prizes, honors, and I won't let anyone pay the bill in a restaurant. I need to learn to receive—that's important. What else? I need at least eight hours of solitude every day, and silence, but that's a virtue, not a fault, because it means that for at least eight hours I'm not bothering anyone. Imagine what those poor creatures' lives would be like if I were retired! I'm jealous, as I told you. Fortunately, I met Willie when he was over fifty and a little short of breath from chasing after women the way he had when he was young. He's given me no cause for jealousy. They say that I'm macho in reverse—that is, as much a feminist as the worst patriarch could be macho.

How does Willie deal with your fame? Once I heard him say that he was married to a legend.

He does fine; we're not at all competitive. My work doesn't affect our private life; no journalists or snoops are allowed in our house; in our small social circle Willie stands out, he's the center of attention. I trail behind him like a shadow. I fit my schedule to his; that way we can be together as much as possible. Willie has a lot of self-confidence; the few times someone has called him Señor Allende, he's laughed. He has no trouble seeing me on a stage or surrounded by photographers; he doesn't feel left out—he realizes it's part of my job, just as arguing in court is part of his role as a lawyer.

I've never seen you trail like a shadow behind *anyone;* on the other hand, I saw him appear on stage in a tux, carrying a bouquet of flowers for you.

But that's very rare. What you're referring to is a talk I gave on the subject of love to raise money for some fellowships. His being there was icing on the cake and he, very gracefully, agreed to do it, but I seldom ask him to do that kind of thing.

In *The Infinite Plan,* the protagonist, Gregory Reeves, grows up in the Latino barrio of Los Angeles, and although he succeeds in escaping that atmosphere of poverty and oppression, he stays in touch with his Hispanic background. Is that like Willie?

Yes, I think that's why he married me. He understands how we are; he speaks perfect Spanish, cooks Mexican dishes, likes boleros, and loves to go to Chile—or any other Latin American country. What he appreciates most is the large family we've formed between the two of us; I think he has wanted a family like this all his life. Willie's not your typical North American. He opens his arms to anyone who comes from south of the border. Ninety percent of his clients are poor, often illegal, Latin immigrants.

You speak of him with admiration, like a bride, but you've been

together more than fourteen years. Hasn't your love changed at all?

Relationships, like everything else, change. They're living organisms that grow, mature, send out tentacles, roots, lose hair, shrink or swell, which is why the couple's ability to adapt to changes at every stage is essential.

Could you fall in love again?

(*Unhesitatingly*) Of course! (*And we both erupt with laughter.*)

Paula

By chance, I saw at close hand how you suffered during the illness and death of your daughter. You often told me during that time that you could not write again, but the fact is that you were writing *Paula,* perhaps your best work. It has been said that *Paula* follows in the best tradition of the novelized memoir.

I wasn't aware that I was writing a book. I began those pages when Paula fell into a coma, and I kept writing all through 1992, when she was ill, first in Madrid and later in California. After her death, when I thought I would never stop crying and never hold a pencil in my hand again, my mother came to my rescue with the idea that I should write. She said there were no antidepressants, therapists, or vacations that could help me, because mourning is a long dark tunnel we must pass through alone. There is light at the other end, she said; keep walking and trust in your life force. And so, day by day, all through 1993, I groped my way through that tunnel. My way of accomplishing that was to write. I rewrote the letter I had begun for my daughter in the hospital in Madrid, and I incorporated bits of the one hundred and ninety letters I had sent to my mother in Chile during that endless year, and that she returned to me; I also referred to the love letters Paula and Ernesto had exchanged during their brief courtship.

Did Paula know she had porfiria?

Yes. Several years before, a cousin of hers who lived in Uruguay became gravely ill, and when her parents saw that she was dying, they took her to a clinic in Houston. After countless examinations, they discovered she was suffering from porfiria, a rare hereditary condition. That explained the death of another cousin and symptoms shared by her aunt, her grandfather, and others of Miguel's relatives. Everyone in the family was given a blood test, and that was how we learned that Miguel and Paula both had porfiria. Nicolás came out negative in the test made in Venezuela. After his sister died, I urged him to repeat the test in the United States, and that time it came out positive. By then he already had two children, and his wife was expecting a third.

What happened to the cousin in Houston?

She recovered completely.

Porfiria is an illness that one can have for a long time without showing any symptoms, and even when they do surface, the patient recovers if given the proper care.

That is usually the case. After *Paula* was published, I received hundreds of letters from people with the disease, especially women. The condition tends to be more serious in them than in men, because hormonal changes often trigger a crisis: puberty, menstruation, pregnancy, giving birth, maternity, menopause, birth control pills, and so on. But if the person is aware of her condition, takes care of herself, and is treated in time, porfiria shouldn't be fatal today.

What a strange illness! It's associated with a king of England. You spent a year at Paula's bedside, several months of that caring for her in your home in California. It seems fairly obvious that in her case there was medical negligence.

No doubt of it, but I don't torture myself thinking about that. I believe it was karma. It was her karma to die young; mine is to live for her, remembering her.

What were you able to do to help her?

Love her very much . . . care for her day and night. It wasn't taxing physically, but emotionally I reached the limits of my strength. There was no other way, Celia. I was the one who should have looked after her, and I wanted to do it. Wouldn't you have done the same? When my daughter was in that coma, she became a baby again, more fragile and vulnerable than even a newborn, because she couldn't cry or move or swallow or communicate pain. Paula returned to my womb, the Paula she was before she was born. I began to live as if she were inside me. It was a natural process, like pregnancy, except that when the time came, we were separated by death, not birth.

After the neurologist explained your daughter's condition, did you have hope for her recovery? (*In 1991, from Spain, Isabel had written me a letter filled with hope; I attach a few paragraphs from it at the end of this chapter.*)

I brought Paula from Spain because, among other reasons, I hoped to find a treatment for her in the United States. But soon I realized that my daughter was beyond any human aid. That was in May of 1992. After a month in a rehabilitation clinic in California, where she went through exhaustive tests, the physicians suggested that we put her in an institution because there was nothing anyone could do. "That way you can go on with your lives," they told me. "She isn't aware of anything." The idea seemed unacceptable to the whole family. We organized a hospital at home, on the first floor, to give Paula the care she needed; I hired three women who took shifts in helping, all Latinas and mothers, so they could speak to her in Spanish and coddle her as they did their own children. The family also took turns, all of us together. We had the help of an exceptional doctor, Cheri Forrester. After she saw Paula and studied the records from the hospital in Madrid and the American clinic, she asked, "What is it you want me to do?" My answer was, "Help me keep her comfortable and calm, free of pain, and, when the time comes, help her die."

What did you know about the pain?

Porfiria crises are terrible. The stomach pain and the anguish can

be unbearable. Along with Ernesto, her husband, we decided that if
there were another attack, we would give her all the morphine needed to prevent suffering, but we also decided that if Paula had an
infection, pneumonia, for example—which often happens with
immobilized patients—we wouldn't treat it, we wouldn't send her
back to the hospital or give her antibiotics; we would let her go off
to the other world in peace.

**You needed a doctor who would be sympathetic to your situa-
tion; not all would.**

Yes, that's true. It wasn't only Paula who was suffering. The entire
family was devastated. I explained to Dr. Forrester that in view of the
fact that conventional science had not been able to help my daughter,
I wanted to try some alternative treatments, and she put me in contact
with Dr. Miki Shima, a specialist in Asian medicine. Then I looked
everywhere for psychics, healers, shamans . . . any miracle available.
Cheri Forrester told me that if it were her daughter, she would do the
same, but that I should set some parameters or my search would
become a vice, an addiction to hope. We decided on a limit of three
months. During that time, I tried everything, including the claims of a
fellow who sold me a magnetized mattress to "move energy," another
who brought flasks of water from a miraculous virgin in Mexico, and
a long-distance psychic who charged a fortune to look at a photo of
Paula and recommend vitamins. In the meanwhile, there was a chain
of people praying for her across three continents. Teresian schools
around the globe joined together to pray for her daily. I'm not a religious person, but I clung to those hopes. Three months later, nothing
had improved. Paula was slowly getting weaker. I had to admit that
nothing, not magnetized mattresses, not Chinese herbs, not gold needles, not telepathic psychics, had worked the hoped-for miracle.

**I remember that year very well; every time I saw you, you were
worse, more torn apart, more sad.**

In September I began to accept that I had many years ahead with
Paula in that state, that it was going to be a very slow and distress-

ing process, that I had to ration my strength or I would die before she did. I had no objective or goal, only the slow trajectory of life toward death. But I clung to her living body. I found a certain happiness in holding her, caring for her, putting her in her wheelchair and taking her out on the terrace to sit in the sun. Then winter came and I couldn't take her outside; after that, we made her comfortable in her heated room and played classical music for her. I would sit beside her and read poems to her, and tell her stories about the past.

Was there any sign from her that she was aware of what you were doing?

Never. Her eyes were growing more and more opaque; every day it was more difficult to perceive any sign. She turned inward, as if one by one she were cutting the threads that tied her to reality and to life. By mid-November I stopped praying she would live and began to pray that she could ease into death. Ernesto, her husband, came from New York to visit her. Every time he came to see his wife, he brought her gifts: perfumes, the sports clothes she liked. . . . It was so moving to see the strength of Ernesto's love for my daughter! He would lay her on the floor, propped up by pillows, and lie down beside her for a nap. They looked like a couple in love, deep asleep, but if you were close you would see the dried tears on my son-in-law's cheeks.

(There is a pause. The recollection overwhelms her. Her voice loses its musical intonation.)

I realized that this man could spend years bound to a woman who was a living corpse. I talked with him, trying to convince him that he must begin to cut the ties between them, to separate himself from her, to start a new life. I explained once again what he knew but his heart refused to accept: that Paula would never regain consciousness, never so much as enjoy the birds and fresh air; that it really didn't matter any longer where she was or whom she was with, since she no longer belonged to this world. Let her go, Ernesto, I begged him; I've been told that when we cling to someone, that person agonizes forever and can't die—it's as if she were chained. Finally, Ernesto, weeping, agreed. The next day we both went to Paula's room, locked the door, took her in our arms, and told her she could leave, that we were fine, that we were going to be all right, that we would always be with her in spirit, that we would never forget her, that she should go now, please, that there was nothing left to keep her in that body and that it was unbearable suffering for all of us to see her trapped like that. From that day on, Paula declined visibly. It may have begun before that, and I simply hadn't wanted to acknowledge it. But I noticed symptoms I hadn't seen before. Six days later, she died.

(*Tears are running down Isabel's cheeks, very quietly. The knot in my throat dissolves into tears. For a long time we sit without speaking.*)

She died on December 6, a Sunday, at four in the morning, exactly one year after falling into a coma. Ernesto had left for China on a lightning business trip. That Saturday, when we realized Paula was dying, we were unable to locate him. We left a telephone message, and when he got back to New York twenty-four hours later, he found our urgent messages and immediately caught a flight to California. Paula had been dead for about thirty hours. During that time, she had lain waiting in her bed, because I wanted Ernesto to be able to tell her goodbye at home. Celia, my daughter-in-law, and I opened all the windows to let in the winter air, and kept the body cool. Bundled in blankets, we sat by Paula's bedside. The children, Alejandro, one and a half, and Andrea, six months, in coats and woolen caps, played nearby. And the cat settled at the foot of Paula's bed, without moving, all that time. Family life went on. What mark will that memorable week-end leave in the hearts of my grandchildren? I don't think it will be a morbid memory; I believe it will leave a layer of profound peace, a realization that life and death are inseparable. (*There is infinite sadness on Isabel's face.*) Paula's name floats in the air; her spirit is always in our memory, in our conversations. When Alejandro is sad, he says he misses Paula. Actually, he's feeling sad about something else—it happens to all of us, even the children—but he doesn't know how to say what's causing him pain. We're very strong in this family—we don't cry easily—but Alejandro has seen us cry for Paula. It may be that he thinks that the only acceptable excuse for crying is the aunt who has gone away forever.

(*Her voice is gentle; she is reaching the end of a prayer.*)

Paula opened a space that allows others to weep out their sorrow. That's what happened with thousands of readers who, after reading the book, wrote you such moving letters.

Sometimes my grandson is sad because he feels insecure, because of his own losses, which he doesn't know how to articulate, and he wraps himself in Paula's memory to cry. That happens to many readers. Here, read this letter that came today. It's from a woman who started reading *Paula* in an airplane. She says that when she got to the airport in Milan, she didn't rush outside to hail a taxi, but sat down to finish the book and cried for hours. Deep down, she was crying for all the losses and abandonment and separations in her life, not for Paula; she was crying over a divorce, her mother's death, many things she hadn't given herself permission to cry about before. Paula opened a floodgate, and an uncontainable river of tears flooded over her in that airport in Milan.

There is something about you I was aware of even before Paula died. In the same way you celebrate life, love, eroticism, you have an eternal, ancestral ritual of union with the dead you have loved. Two scenes in your books have moved me powerfully: one is when Clara is preparing Férula's corpse. Férula has only a hair or two left on her head; she has become a human ruin living in the wretched little room where she died poor and abandoned. Clara washes her corpse, grooms her, talks to her about the family, says goodbye the way you said goodbye to Paula. Eva Luna does the same with Zulema after she commits suicide by putting a pistol in her mouth; she bathes her, combs her hair, lays her out, makes her presentable so she can be seen by her husband. In these times and in this North American culture we live in, such tender care of the dead is inconceivable. Where did this sense of devotion come from?

I don't know. I never saw it. I imagined it in my books. Oh! I did experience it a little when my mother-in-law died, a woman I loved very much. When someone you love dies, it takes a while to say goodbye to their body, and all these rituals help us accept the death; it's a kind of transition, a last farewell before being parted. It's so hard just to say "All right, the body is gone, now we have to invent a purely spiritual relationship." My mother-in-law was a pure soul, transparent, an innocent, absolute love. She died in a hospital in Uruguay in 1978. It was a very dark moment in my life. My marriage with Miguel was a disaster; I was in love with a musician and was planning to follow him to Spain, but my mother-in-law fell gravely ill and I flew to tell her goodbye. It was dusk as I arrived at the hospital. My exhausted sister-in-law had gone home to rest for a while; she hadn't left her mother's side for several days. When I got there, they were moving my mother-in-law from intensive care to a private room where she could die undisturbed. I stayed with her all that night; at some moment I lay down on the bed with her and began to tell her about her grandchildren, whom she adored and hadn't seen in more than two years, about our life in Venezuela, about Miguel's work. I didn't, of course, mention how badly our marriage was going; I talked only about good things and how much we missed her, and how life hadn't been the same since we had been separated from her, about how she had been the center of Paula's and Nicolás's lives. I showed her photos of the children. She was in a coma, bleeding internally, but maybe her spirit absorbed that happy news.

Did she respond?

No, she was completely unconscious. The doctor came at dawn and told me she had only a few hours to live. Then I remembered that no one had called Miguel in Venezuela. I ran to look for a telephone and told him he had to catch the first flight he could find, because his mother was waiting for him to come so she could die. I thought he might not get there in time, but at least he could accompany his father and his sister in their grief. My mother-in-law lived all that day; she waited for her son to arrive, and died twenty minutes later. I suppose that that night beside my mother-in-law, and the time I spent later with her body, inspired the passages in *The House of the*

Spirits and *Eva Luna* when Clara and Eva pay their intimate last homage to the corpses of Férula and Zulema. The night Paula died, Celia and I performed those intimate ceremonies as if we had done them many times: we chose Paula's clothing, arranged the room, placed photos of the children on her breast, so she would always have them. We made a small pagan altar, we lighted candles, we set flowers everywhere, we did the things old, mourning-clad women do in Greece to help the dying, then dress the body and weep and wail at the burial. We repeated the age-old rites inscribed in genetic memory. Just as we women know instinctively what to do when giving birth, so we know how to face death. My relationship with my ex-daughter-in-law, Celia, is marked by three essential happenings: the births of my two grandchildren, which I witnessed, helping them from Celia's womb, and Paula's transition toward death, a time Celia was there to help *me*. That created an elemental bond between us.

There are people who feel you trivialized your personal tragedy by making a public display of such personal sorrow. Did you gain some consolation from that?

A student once asked me if I didn't feel vulnerable after telling all my secrets. I told her no, that I felt much stronger. Secrets are debilitating, truth strengthens us. In sharing that experience with others, I learned that I am not alone in my suffering—everyone has his or her own burden. That isn't a consolation in itself, but it makes me more humble and helps me resign myself to the trials fate sets before me.

As you were speaking, I realized that you have lived everything to the fullest: happiness, passion, success, love, pain, sisterhood. You have absorbed everything life has to give.

To give and to take away. When things happen to us, we face them any way we can, blindly, clawing, without a plan, without elegance . . . the analysis comes much later. Sometimes fate leads us to dead-end streets where there is no way out and no choice but just to plunge in. Pregnancy is a good metaphor. We are nine months with something growing in our womb, inexorably growing. There is noth-

ing to be gained by complaining that you're getting fat, that your legs
are swelling, that you're vomiting; those nine months march on . . .
until it's time to give birth. Then you hold the baby in your arms, and
you offer him your breast, and, if you're lucky, you will watch him
grow up . . . or if you're very unlucky, you may see him die. That's
how I feel about my life. It's a natural process, painful and uncom-
fortable at times, at other times marvelous. It's a road we can't travel back; we can only move forward toward our death, day after day.
Later we rearrange the past, tricking memory.

How do you mean?

We remember only what we want to keep: the most brilliant, the
darkest tones. The gray shades are lost. Memory, like fiction, moves
from revelation to revelation.

Letter to Celia Correas Zapata from Isabel Allende
Madrid, January 1992

I am taking advantage of a few quiet hours to write you,
even though it takes letters so long to arrive that by the time
you receive this one, Paulita will be dancing flamenco and this
nightmare will be behind us.

Willie came to see me, and his visit has been good for me.
I am reminded that I have a life outside this hospital where I
have spent every day and night of December, and now part of
January. I have a husband, a son, a grandson, friends, the California sun and a house waiting for me, with things I love and
flowers I planted. Somewhere there is happiness. . . . I had
thought I would never be able to make love again, to laugh or
enjoy a good wine, which something irreparable had broken
inside me. That isn't true.

I have Paula with me always, as in the days I was carrying
her in my womb, a constant and marvelous presence. I try not
to see her only as she is, so sick, but remember her laughing,
her hair blowing in the wind, see the pretty girl she was and
will be again. I am filled with a kind of certainty that she will

get well, that she will go to the United States with her husband, and that one day in the not-too-distant future, she will be looking through the window at the bridges in San Francisco Bay. She may be in a wheelchair, but that seems so unimportant. . . . How we distort priorities and values in a tragedy like this! I pray only that she will live, that she will get out of intensive therapy, that she will breathe on her own again, without daring to think of the months or years that will follow, terrible days when she will have to fight with all her heart to win the smallest victories. One day she will move a hand, another she will smile again, and, like a baby, she will have to learn everything anew. One of the most terrifying aspects of porfiria is that a third of the patients who recover from a crisis like Paula's are left with mental problems. They experience a systemic depression difficult to treat, because they can't take drugs. Hallucinations, suicidal tendencies, melancholy. I hope we may escape that; my poor daughter has already suffered enough.

Sometimes I am afraid. How could this have happened to us? These dramas happen to other people . . . always to someone else! Sometimes my mother and I talk about how lucky we have been in our family; violence and death have been circling around us always, nipping at our heels, but never touched us. We have always slipped away just ahead of disaster, but we escaped. Now grief won't let us go. I feel as if I'm going to die, that I can't draw air into my lungs. I pray heaven to give Paula my energy and my health. I have lived forty-nine years, and I have done everything anyone can do. What more is there? Why her and not me?

With Paulita's illness, everything has changed. Willie and I are separated; you can't imagine how painful that is to us, but there's no alternative. He can't leave his work, and I will spend the year here in Madrid. We'll travel back and forth, but no matter how often we do that, it won't be enough. We found each other very late in our lives; that's why we had planned never to be apart, but sometimes we aren't in control of anything. Fate plays a prank and leaves us pointed in a new direction. I think about Ernesto, who loves Paulita so much. He told me that he misses her, that he needs her, that without her the house is an empty hole. That man will have to be very strong and very patient because it will be a very long time until he gets back the woman he married.

Grief is a strange thing; it's like a necessary apprenticeship. Without grief we don't truly grow. At first you defend yourself; you kick, resist, deny, reject, get angry, but the grief persists; and in the end it always gets the upper hand. If you're strong, and if you're lucky, it will bend you but not break you. There comes a moment that you accept it; you realize, slowly, that there is no possible escape and that you must drink the last bitter dregs from that cup. You simply suffer, with no relief, and you reach the bottom; then you give a kick and begin to rise toward the surface. I know that that moment will come for me; that is how it has been before in my life. But I am still in the stage of denial and rejection—that's why the pain is so bad. If I could open up and absorb it like a sponge, without putting up any resistance, it would invade me, penetrate every crevice, soak through me, and then start receding. It would leave bruises, scars, and memories, but it would go away. Ernesto has great natural wisdom; he accepts what has happened and is calm in his suffering; I have never seen him rebel. Just the opposite, he tells me not to agonize so, that everything that happens is for the best, and that I should place myself in God's hands. There are persons like Ernesto, but little people like me have no faith in God, or in themselves, and they have to absorb many blows before they learn the indispensable lessons. This is a slow road toward knowledge, repeatedly tripping over the same stones, but finally one may reach old age with some wisdom.

During this time I have learned that love is the only thing that truly matters. Paula sowed affection throughout her life, and now it is being harvested for her and for me as well. It's so moving to know how many people love my daughter. My Paulita! Oh, Celia, when will all this end? What lies ahead for us? I can't take any more. . . .

Isabel Allende in California in 1991. (Photo courtesy of Isabel Allende)

Isabel Allende's daughter, Paula and son-in-law, Ernesto at their wedding in 1990. (Photo courtesy of Isabel Allende)

Isabel Allende's son, Nicolás and his wife, Lori. (Photo courtesy of Isabel Allende)

Isabel Allende with her three grandchildren: Andrea, Alejandro and Nicole, 1994. (Photo courtesy of Isabel Allende)

Isabel Allende at Barcelona Universidad, 1998. (Photo courtesy of Isabel Allende)

Isabel Allende at Barcelona Universidad, 1998. (Photo courtesy of Isabel Allende)

Isabel Allende in Madrid, 2000. (Photo courtesy of Isabel Allende)

Isabel Allende's mother and Tío Ramón at her presentation of *Retrato en Sepia* in Madrid, 2000. (Photo courtesy of Isabel Allende)

From left to right: Celia, Roland, Willie, and Isabel.

A Latino magazine for the new millennium

el ANDAR

SPRING 1999

CLINTON: EL AMANTE
INCONCLUSO
GABRIEL
GARCÍA
MÁRQUEZ

GATE OF PLEASURE
ROSARIO
FERRÉ
*Las caderas
del encanto*

EXCLUSIVE

ISABEL
ALLENDE

and Celia Zapata

*Las comadres discuss
testosterone, politics
and humor*

VIGILANTE
BORDER WAR

$4.95 U.S./$5.95 Canada

Celia Correas Zapata and Isabel Allende on the cover of *el Andar,*
1999. (Photo courtesy of *el Andar* Publications)

Of Children and Books

Hear these words,
they come blazing with feeling
and if not for me
would not be spoken.

Pablo Neruda

Tata once had a sweetheart, also named Rosa, who died in mysterious circumstances. It was never learned absolutely whether she died of poison, like Rosa in *The House of the Spirits*, but it is a fact that Tata married Rosa's younger sister, Isabel Barros Moreira, the grandmother to whom Isabel owes her name. That grandmother never abandoned her. "I wrote without effort, without thinking, because my clairvoyant grandmother was dictating to me," says Isabel, who still believes that the spirits of her grandparents came to her in Caracas to dictate the family history. I met Isabel and her grandparents at the same time, because she sets their photographs on the night table as she takes possession of her hotel room wherever she is traveling. Although in 1981 she was working twelve hours a day as an administrative secretary in a private school, when Isabel got home she sat down and wrote on her portable typewriter until dawn of the following day. In that trance-like state she felt no fatigue and needed no sleep. "[I]t was as if I had a lighted flame inside me."

The letter to her grandfather began to grow longer in a way she had never foreseen; the weight of the tote in which she carried the manuscript with her everywhere increased apace, to such a point that when she decided to count the pages, she found she had five hundred, "whited out so many times with correction fluid that some were stiff as cardboard; others were stained with soup or had glued-in sections that unfolded like maps." Isabel did not yet know that she had begun to fulfill her destiny, but she felt the magnitude of the work she was bringing to light with genesis-like shudders. "I was as solicitous of that ribbon-tied pile of pages as I would be for a newborn baby."

She finished writing *The House of the Spirits*, in Caracas, near Christmastime. I have asked her many times if she felt something different that night in 1981 when she wrote the words *The End*. "It was in my bedroom, where I had taken the typewriter while Miguel was sleeping, in the early morning." She told me that she wrote those last words after a dream in which Tata helped her resolve the ending that had been giving her so much trouble. She closed up the typewriter, tied up the manuscript with the usual ribbon, put it in her tote, turned out the light, and went to bed.

"The epilogue was the most difficult part; I wrote it many times, without finding the tone I wanted; it seemed sentimental, or sounded like a sermon or political tract. I knew what I wanted to tell but didn't know how to express it, until once again ghosts came to my aid." She saw her dead grandfather in the dream, in the same room she had tiptoed into to steal Memé's silver mirror, and she sat down beside him to tell him the story she had just written; as she was talking with him, the shadows dissipated and the room was filled with light. She realized then that the solution was to let Alba tell the story. "Alba, the granddaughter, is writing the story of her family beside the body of her grandfather, Esteban Trueba, who is to be buried the next morning."

Isabel had been a journalist, the author of stories for children, plays, and scripts for radio and television, never daring to admit her true vocation as a writer. When she finished *The House of the Spirits,* she hadn't the remotest sense of the gigantic step she had taken, or of where she was headed. "I did not know those pages would change my life, but I felt that a long period of paralysis and muteness had ended."

Joy for the author's triumph was unanimous in the families of

Isabel and Miguel Frías. It was some time before they saw the first edition of *La casa de los espíritus*, published by Plaza y Janés in Spain, which finally reached Caracas through the good offices of Tío Ramón. Then came publicity tours and the first contacts with European editors.

For several years, Isabel's marriage with Miguel had been one long, courteous endeavor to live together in peace. Passion had died years before; what was left between them was a cordial understanding. Celebration over the triumph of *The House of the Spirits* was soon erased when Miguel lost his job and began to suffer fainting spells. It was then that doctors discovered that Miguel and Paula shared the same genetic condition: porfiria. It wasn't cause for immediate alarm. With minimal precautions, sufferers of porfiria can live a normal life. The gulf widened between Isabel and Miguel. "It was impossible to confront a husband who offered no resistance." Years earlier, when Isabel had followed the Argentine flautist "in an hypnotic trance, like the mice of Hamelin," only to return three months later because she couldn't live without her children, it was Miguel's thought—perhaps due to British phlegm—that they should go on living together as if nothing had happened. "That blindness in the face of reality was the strongest facet of his character," Isabel wrote in *Paula*.

The end was inevitable. The definitive separation took place without any grand recriminations; after twenty-four years of marriage, Isabel Allende was again free. By then she had published three books: *The House of the Spirits, Of Love and Shadows,* and *Eva Luna.*

Isabel is first of all a mother. She loves her children with a conscious and total love she learned from her mother, but a more joyful love, free of the veils of sadness that enveloped her own childhood. Before Paula was born, almost as soon as she was conceived, Isabel saw her in a dream. Just as between Isabel and her mother, a secret communication developed between mother and daughter when Isabel was carrying Paula in her womb. She told her, "Those months you were inside me were a time of perfect happiness. I have never again felt so closely accompanied."

Pía Leiva, Isabel's close Chilean friend, remembers Isabel's feverish activity before birthday parties, how she created toys, decorations, paintings, costumes, books dedicated to her children, puppet theaters, pantomimes, parades—everything hatched from her ingenuity or made with her own hands to make her children happy.

"My children determined my life; since the day they were born, I have never thought of myself as an individual but as part of an inseparable trio . . . it never occurred to me that motherhood was an option; I considered it inevitable, like the seasons."

The documentary film based on *Paula,* produced by the BBC and narrated by Isabel, was made possible because she and her mother, Panchita, had through the years collected photographs of Paula, along with her favorite belongings, in a kind of sanctuary. Everything was kept intact despite moves, travels, and changes in the lives of all the family. The photos were safeguarded like relics; through them march the children in different phases: as newborns, Isabel in a white dressing gown, weary but victorious, holding her trophy in her arms after the delivery; Paula and Nicolás as children in grade school, the period during which they appeared in Isabel's stories as Juanita and Perico; family parties at graduation time; the wedding day; the grandchildren.

This woman who is so sensitive to love can't help seeing the similarity that exists between creating a child and creating a book. "The happy process of engendering a child, the patience during the long gestation, the strength to bring it into the world, the feeling of profound astonishment at the fruition, I can compare only to creating a book. Children, like books, are voyages into oneself, in which body, mind, and soul take a new direction, turn toward the very center of existence."

In October of 1987, Isabel came to California at the invitation of the Poetry Center and the Department of Foreign Languages at San Jose State University in California. She left behind her a wake of laughter and joy, of enthusiasm and affection among students and professors, an alliance that has strengthened, not faded, with the years. Isabel has been marked by a strange destiny that demands she keep wandering to fulfill her fate, that she was to return time and time again to San Jose, the starting point for her years in the United States, where the most decisive part of her life will be lived.

There was a fortuitous meeting on this first trip, and when Isabel met Willie Gordon, she became the heroine and protagonist of a love story. Many years have passed, and the union between them has been put to an unrelenting series of tests. Like a well-tempered bell, it continues to reverberate with the same clarity it had the first time it was struck, when their eyes met in the Hotel Fairmont in San Jose. Neither the tragedies of Paula and Jennifer, daughters prematurely dead, nor problems with Willie's other children, nor Isabel's difficulties in adapting to the United States, have succeeded in dulling the mettle of the love that unites them. "Together we have the strength of a racing train," Isabel has written.

"It was like being born again; I could invent a fresh version of myself only for this man." When they met, Isabel already had three published novels and was internationally acclaimed, with translations of her books in more than twenty-eight different languages. Although Willie had read *De amor y de sombra* two months before first meeting Isabel in San Jose, and undoubtedly had entered her world before she entered his, the attraction between them was an immediate electric charge.

"What was my life like before Willie? It was a good life, too, filled with intense emotions. I have lived the extremes; few things have been easy or smooth for me . . . storming the bastion with sword in hand, without an instant's truce—or boredom; great successes and smashing failures, passions and loves, but also loneliness, work, losses, desertions." In her column *Los impertinentes,* anticipating the future, Isabel revealed a positive idea of American husbands when she wrote: "This is one of few examples of a man who washes the dishes, plays with the children, and mows the lawn on Saturday."

This experience of married and domestic life in California was to be very different from that of her first marriage. Nothing augured well for that new life: the atmosphere, the language, the personality of Willie, who loved her but did not lend himself to being subjugated, Willie's youngest son still at home and the two older children constantly getting into difficulties—a mass of adverse circumstances coalesced around her to discourage her. Nonetheless, this battler who has spent a lifetime "in the bullring" would not be crushed, and did what she had done in Caracas when life in her house became intolerable: she wrote. Armed for war, with a machete in one hand and a pencil case in the other, she wrote *The Stories of Eva Luna* in Willie's law office in the heart of San Francisco. Once the domestic landscape was reasonably peaceful, she continued with *The Infinite Plan*, the novelized life of the man she loved in the character of Gregory Reeves. When Willie saw the book published for the first time, he felt his love was sanctified. He has told me that it was one of the happiest moments of his life.

In 1991, work, patience, and love began to bear tangible fruit. Her children, Paula, and then Nicolás, were married in Caracas, shortly after her own ceremony in California; all three had simultaneously fallen victim to amorous madness. Paula settled in Spain with Ernesto, a young, loving couple, like any other, looking forward to a long and productive life, with grandchildren for Isabel to spoil. On December 6, 1991, when Isabel was launching *El Plan Infinito* in Spain, she received an urgent call; it was about her daughter Paula.

Paula's last conscious words were "I love you, Mama." Whether because of error or fate, Paula fell into a coma and remained in a vegetative state in the hospital in Madrid for six months, and then six months more in the family home in San Rafael, California, under her mother's care. When Isabel saw her daughter's body assaulted by tubes, needles, and probes, connected night and day to a respirator, she refused to be bowed by the illness. She took her daughter from the hospital in Madrid as soon as she could breathe on her own, and installed an intensive care unit on board a passenger plane to the United States. Paula never emerged from her coma. Those were months of studying Paula's staring eyes, trying to glimpse a cause for hope. On Sunday, June 15, 1994, after reading the manuscript of *Paula*, I wrote a very emotional note to Isabel. "From the time of the letter you wrote me on a flight to Madrid, I have been close to your project of helping Paula recover, and have shared the expectations for her return to your world, to our world, the only world we know. As I read your manuscript, I, who already knew the ending, wore a kind of merciful blindfold that allowed me to join with you in your hope, and, even knowing that there would be no salvation, I let you lead me along the path of the impossible, of the miracle." It takes superhuman strength to see a daughter beyond the loving reach of her mother. What is the connection between that inert figure and the slender girl overflowing with impetuous goodness? "Oh, your grace, Paula," Isabel would utter in a grieving voice as she contemplated the state in which her daughter lay.

We all expected a miracle. In Paula's expressions, Isabel thought she saw signs of inner life struggling to be expressed. Isabel, invincible gladiator, sovereign of dreams, tender and sensitive mother, a woman filled with redemptive energy, attempted to establish a pact with the creator that would allow Paula to live through her. "Can I live in your stead? Carry you in my body that you can recover the fifty or sixty years stolen from you? I don't mean remember you, but live your life, be you, let you love and feel and breathe in me, let my gestures be yours, my voice your voice. Let me be erased, dissolved, so that you take possession of my body, oh, Paula, so that your inexhaustible and joyful goodness may completely replace my lifelong fears, my paltry ambitions, my depleted vanity."

Paula is more than a memoir; it is a long prayer. Rising in unison are Isabel's beloved spirits, and, just as when they dictated *The House of the Spirits* into her ear, their voices blend into a single note of harmonious concert in their elegy. Isabel goes forth to meet death and converts it into an ally of life, immortalizing the spirit of her daughter. In a letter written by Paula during her honeymoon in Scotland, to be opened after her death, she asks that she not be forgotten. In writing *Paula*, the mother is fulfilling her daughter's last wish. The book reunites us with Paula the woman and, as in a hierophantic ceremony that in every repetition conserves its sacredness, we are again with her every time we read those pages. In a final message, Paula brings each of us close to the spirits of our dead and to our faraway, living, loved ones. There is a single light that allows us to see in the penumbra of both worlds: love.

Isabel said during Paula's long agony: "This is a road I must travel bleeding," and she refused to anesthetize herself with tranquilizers or sleeping pills. When she asked herself where Paula was before her birth, and where she would be after she died, *doña* Panchita, Isabel's mother, replied, "Paula is already in God. God is what binds, what holds together the fabric of life . . . what you call love."

It is true, Isabel. Paula performed subtle miracles, as you once said; she forced us to grow and taught us the paths of compassion and wisdom.

Aphrodite

Let's talk about *Aphrodite*. When she read the manuscript, our translator, Margaret Sayers Peden, said it was a fascinating mixture of historical research, psychological truths, humor, and fiction. In this book, through sensuality, you recapture your taste for life following your long mourning over Paula's death. It seems a return to a conscious, slightly spiritual sensuality, though that may sound paradoxical. Tell me about this return to sensuality.

This book began almost as a joke with Robert Shekter, a friend whom I often met in the morning for coffee. We had this idea for a book I could write on aphrodisiacs, using specific recipes, with his illustrations. But once I began to do a little research, I soon found myself immersed in the vast and passionate theme of sensuality and food. I began laughing again; I rediscovered the pleasure of play, of irony, of free-flowing narration that I had nearly forgotten in recent years. I asked Carmen Balcells what she thought about the idea, and her enthusiasm gave me confidence to go ahead. I wrote nearly three hundred pages, Robert Shekter produced his drawings, and my mother, in Chile, created more than a hundred recipes, guided by a list of aphrodisiac ingredients I sent her, and then she came to my house in California to test them. This book drew me out of the very long, dark tunnel I had been in for three years. At last I again saw the world in all its extravagant incongruities and beauty.

This turn toward nonfiction reveals a kind of special maturity, one not very common among women writers, who seldom are

essayists, to say nothing of essayists with humor.

They haven't had the chance. A woman writer has to win respect very circumspectly.

From my reading of *Aphrodite,* I can say that it is a humorous, well-documented, meditative, reflective text. What I like best is that you make us laugh, the way you did when you were just beginning.

How can you be serious writing about eroticism and aphrodisiacs? I laughed writing it, I hope others smile as they read it.

There are unforgettable passages on love, passion, and tenderness in your books. Sensual delight is present in all of them, especially *Aphrodite*. After so many pages dedicated to erotic art and aphrodisiacs, what conclusions have you reached?

After two round-the-world circuits of the senses, I discovered that the one aphrodisiac that really works is love.

Love and passion: two constants in your work. At the beginning of *The Stories of Eva Luna,* there is a long, very sensual scene between Rolf Carlé and Eva Luna; it sets the scene for their love affair and for the stories she will tell in the rest of the book. When Irene Beltrán and Francisco come together in *Of Love and Shadows,* love is exalted. That night near the mine of Los Riscos, the torrent of Francisco's lovemaking "washes her into gentle seas." What woman hasn't dreamed of being loved like that? There is a blend of urgent passion and great tenderness in your characters.

Oh, the senses! To smell, touch, taste . . . I'm fascinated by textures, colors, aromas, sounds, flavors. I want my characters to relate to their reality through the senses. It is in those sensually perceived details that the book's universe acquires credibility for the readers. Sometimes they tell me, "It's as if I myself were living it." That's what it's all about, that fiction be perceived as reality. That's why eroticism is important in fiction.

Is *Aphrodite* an essay on sexuality and sensuality?

Essay is a word that frightens me. Let's say that it is musings on pleasure. Eroticism derives from sensuality; the two are inseparable. Sexuality, in contrast, can exist independently of either, as an act of pure brutality. In this book, it's sensuality that interests me.

Why didn't you revert to fiction, which is your forte?

There are so many anecdotes and stories in *Aphrodite* that it might as well be fiction. My agent, Carmen Balcells, says my entire life is fiction.

I like the title; it insinuates sexual gratifications and pleasures.

I'm going to use that phrase for publicity! I want to go back to the novel because I'm attracted by long-term projects that eat up life; it's like falling in love. Some people prefer my short stories, but I think I'm best at the novel.

Are there any autobiographical elements in the love scenes of your novels, or in *Aphrodite*?

If I were a man, I would tell you that it's all autobiographical, and that there's a lot I haven't told but am keeping quiet for the sake of discretion. Haven't you noticed how men preen themselves on this subject? And writers are the worst. Once at a convention of librarians where I was giving the opening address, someone asked me that same question. It was an older, weary, obese woman like many others in the audience. I said that the torrid scenes were pure invention. There was a huge sigh of relief throughout the hall.

Was that an honest answer?

Let's say it was a compassionate one. I didn't want those good women to go away with the idea that life had deprived them of something it had given me with open hands—which itself is not entirely true. Most of the time I describe eroticism *as I would like it to be*. I've been fortunate, and I've called on my own experience at times, but I'm no expert on the Kama Sutra, and flirtation isn't my strong point. In erotic matters I think I fall just about in the middle. There are autobiographical elements in everything I write; if I hadn't experienced fear, love, sorrow, passion, desire—an infinite range of emotions—how could I describe them? In love scenes, I sometimes recount something I've experienced, though maybe only in fantasy.

So where does that leave us? You've lived them or you've imagined them?

I've lived them and I've embroidered them. Rather richly. (*She laughs.*) I tend to invent virtues the lover doesn't have, and if I'm in love, I forgive a lot. I close my eyes and imagine that he's a much better lover than he is in real life. But I'm not complaining. I've had some truly brilliant moments in love, moments I recall with nostalgia and gratitude, and that I use in my novels.

It's comforting to me that a grandmother in the fifth decade of her life would be writing about sensuality, as you do in *Aphrodite*.

Who has more authority to speak on the subject than someone with half a century behind her? Unfortunately, we live in this society in which women are not forgiven their age, Celia. Men are, as long as they have money or power. In other cultures, age is appreciated; wrinkles are worn with pride—they indicate experience, maybe even wisdom. But here we women become invisible the minute we show a gray hair; no one looks at us or listens to us. No one is interested in us except women our own age. Nevertheless, we carry the same fire inside we always have, but instead of using it in games of seduction, we turn it into tremendous curiosity about the world and a desire to learn and be helpful. We can transform ourselves into generous, radiant guardian witches. And we can also be passionate and wise lovers. Why not? Someone told Gloria Steinem that she didn't look sixty, and she replied without missing a beat, "This is how sixty looks!" So when anyone says to me, after reading *Aphrodite*, that it doesn't sound as if it had been written by a fifty-year-old grandmother, I will say, like Gloria, "This is how fifty *is!*"

In *Aphrodite* you use a phrase that really made me laugh: that the only good thing about virginity is losing it. That openness is rare in a Latina. You've written about your own sexuality in very frank terms. Aren't you afraid of the public's negative reaction, most of all, other women's?

No. Women readers usually identify with the foolish things I write about because we've all experienced them. I think that my sexuality has gone through several stages; it has something to do with hormones. Between the ages of fifteen and forty, we're in our full reproductive phase; it isn't at all strange to find us acting like animals in heat. Until I was thirty-five, I was almost Victorian; after that, my curiosity was awakened and I decided to explore a little. After forty-five, I became more selective; quality was more important to me than quantity or variety. I was in luck, because Willie appeared and it was no longer necessary to go hunting men across the planet. Several friends my age announce with pride that they have no interest in sex, although they admit that they would enjoy companionship and tenderness. They say that when obsession ends, it is replaced with a great freedom and creative strength. I read the other day that the best-kept secret in the world is that half the male population becomes impotent around the age of sixty. How many do you know who own up to that?

None. There are two very contradictory situations I find intriguing in *The House of the Spirits*. Clara's apparent incapacity, in the beginning, to fall in love with Esteban Trueba and yet her ability to accept physical, sexual love so naturally. Then, too, the intensity of the love between Blanca and Pedro Tercero: her

determination to get out of the house and live that love on the sly. Do you think that women can find the strength within themselves to carry on a great clandestine love affair?

Celia, don't try to explain everything. In my novels, as in me-the-person, there are many contradictions. I think that women and men are equally able to carry on an affair and lie about it. I grew up with the idea that love can do anything; don't forget that the legend of my mother's and Tío Ramón's love marked my childhood. In a country where there is no divorce, in a Catholic and conservative atmosphere with powerful and closed families, that couple overcame all obstacles with the strength of their passion. Pure passion, like that in novels, because they are not two people who complement one another, two soulmates who find one another in the crucible of the universe; in truth, I'm surprised that, having so little in common, they've lived together half a century. But from somewhere they drew strength to defy half the world and preserve their relationship. Maybe there isn't all that much difference between love and passion.

Every great love begins that way, passionately.

What a shame that tumultuous ardor turns into tranquil love! What I like is the tumult.

In a situation in which two people fall in love, are there insuperable obstacles that can inflame or extinguish passion?

What does inflame passion? One's own fantasy, I suppose. What extinguishes it? Routine, if one is careless, and poverty, certainly. I think that obstacles like distance, class differences, age, race, stepchildren—everything—can be overcome, but an obstacle like conscience destroys passion for me. If I feel guilty, I carry my enemy within me, and finally it gains the upper hand. That's why long-term infidelity doesn't work for me; deceit ruins my pleasure.

For Love

The moment has come to talk about the pied piper of Hamelin, your flautist. You wrote in *Paula* that in 1978, in Caracas, while still married to Miguel, you fell in love with an Argentine musician. You describe, rather ironically, that he played the flute in bed.

That wasn't a metaphor in questionable taste; in fact, that was his instrument, the flute.

Like the one in the story you loved as a child?

Yes, and I followed him blindly to Spain, like those poor mice of Hamelin. Things went rather badly in that adventure, but I couldn't help myself. It would have been worse to spend the rest of my life nursing the frustration that I had had True Love—in caps— right under my nose, but lacked the courage to follow it.

Was it True Love?

Of course not. If it had been, I wouldn't be here today, but I had to discover that for myself. It was pointless for anyone to warn me about it. The effervescence of the passion counteracted the most basic good sense.

Has that happened to you at other times?

Falling in love? Yes, but I learned something in Hamelin, and now I don't trail after the first musician who comes tooting his flute under my window.

If someone wanted to classify you by calling you the quintessential author of love, would you accept that?

Dangerous, I think. Saying "author of love" smacks of the romance novel, and there is nothing farther from that than the twisted relationships among my characters.

But love is one of the major themes in your work, as it no doubt is in your life.

Several themes are repeated in my books: love, death, solidarity, violence, as well as politics, social questions, dreams, coincidences, historical elements. But you're right. Love has been the principal motivation in my life—not just erotic love, of course. Maybe what upholds love is sympathy. A climate of sympathy, affection, intimacy, is like good soil in which everything grows effortlessly. When I say "make love," I'm talking about an encounter that may or may not include sex; it is shared communication, solidarity, affectionate caresses, humor. You could say I "make love" with my grandchildren.

Celia, your daughter-in-law so dear to you, divorced your son under rather difficult conditions. She fell in love with someone else, and for a while it seemed that the family you had worked so hard to bring together had suffered an irreparable rupture. Let's say there was a scandal. How do you feel about that?

I defend my family, and we all suffered over what happened, but I still love my ex-daughter-in-law.

That's admirable. This is the kind of situation that breeds bad blood within families.

I don't even hate Pinochet. Hating is hard work. To hate you have to have a good memory and time to waste. I still love Celia like a daughter for the same reasons I loved her before; she is still the same human being. She hurt some people, but she didn't do it with malice—she couldn't help herself. She acted in the heat of passion. How could I not understand, since I've done the same?

Do you believe that love justifies human acts that harm other defenseless persons?

It depends on the circumstances; each of us must look into her own heart. It isn't up to me to judge.

My father always said that it was better to leave a guilty man free than to lay blame on someone innocent.

No one carries truth around in his pocket. Being tolerant makes for fewer mistakes than being overly virtuous.

We might say that your mother has been a great source of security for you in questions of love.

It may be easy for me to love others because my mother has loved me so much. By receiving so much, I learned to give; they say that's something acquired in childhood.

Loving one's neighbor is very difficult. A Pharisee asked Jesus what was the most important part of his message, and he replied: "Love God, and love your neighbor as you love yourself." You live love, but what do you do when you don't like someone?

I avoid him. There are certain human characteristics that make me very suspicious: adulation, superiority, intolerance, for example.

There are people who talk about love but don't know how to use it; they can't really get close to another human being. Was there someone in your family who had a great capacity for love?

I like to think that my grandmother had it, but she died young. My character would be very different if I'd had an entertaining and affectionate grandmother who loved me unconditionally.

When I think about your grandmother, I see Meryl Streep in the film.

You aren't the only one. There are members of my family who keep photos of Meryl Streep and Jeremy Irons on the piano instead of pictures of my grandparents. The power of film is amazing. My grandmother was small, and she had dark eyes and hair, very different from Meryl Streep.

Was your grandmother like Clara, sweet and calm, sometimes a little vague?

Yes, but she was often depressed and melancholy, and had sudden fits of sarcasm and humor. The material world bored her, and her curiosity about the Beyond was so strong that she died rather young; she couldn't resist the lure of the abyss, of death. With time she grew more and more spiritual; she let go of reality, and finally, she simply wasn't there.

You have a tendency to be spiritual, at times a little mystical. You see that in the last chapters before Paula's death.

Sometimes when I've been holed up a long time writing, I have to make an effort to return to reality. We were talking about the ability to love. We always talk about how much we love, but only rarely do we mention how much we have been loved. I've been given a lot of love. No man has ever left me; doesn't that seem like incredible good luck? I haven't had to kill anyone because of jealousy or rejection.

That's difficult for me to believe. I grew up listening to tangos and reading Bécquer. All love is supposed to end badly. You have a lot of confidence in yourself. Is there any area in which you feel insecure?

Many. My height, for example. I don't go to cocktail parties because all I see are people's nose hairs. And literature, too; I've learned nothing in fifteen years; with each book I have to start again from zero, inventing everything all over again. And life in general; I'm always afraid I will take a misstep and hurt another person.

On a scale of 1 to 10, what grade would you give yourself as a writer, a wife, a mother, a grandmother?

To give myself a grade, I'd have to compare myself to others, and frankly, that isn't worth the trouble—I always come out losing. Motherhood has determined all the important decisions in my life, but priorities change at different stages. At my age, I'm more grandmother than mother. There are days that I'm more lover than writer, but when I'm finishing a novel, I divorce myself from reality, to the point of asking Willie his name, because all I see are shadows. Some time ago, as I was putting the finishing touches on *Aphrodite*, my four-year-old granddaughter started crying because I was so absorbed at my computer that I wasn't speaking to her. Her brother, who is two years older, consoled her, saying, "Leave her alone. She'll get over it soon, she's imagining. . . ."

You've never held back; that's a sign of great courage. There are people who choose not to love because they don't want to suffer. Let's go back to your lover, whom apparently, we are turning into a universal archetype, a mysterious fellow like the lover in *La última niebla* [The Last Fog]. (*Isabel laughs.*) You could have chosen not to follow him to Spain. At that moment you knew that serious consequences could result from that choice, yet you followed the impulse of your passion. You could have stayed in Chile after the military coup, not gone to Venezuela, where you went through some difficult times, but you didn't want your children to grow up in a dictatorship. Going to Venezuela meant completely uprooting your life, but you made that choice without fear. For years you tried to save a marriage that was dying, and yet, when the moment came to separate, you faced it head on and

resolved it within a few hours. Just as you assume the problems of your children and your grandchildren, death and birth. You could have placed Paula in a hospital, sparing yourself the constant pain of watching your daughter slowly dying—that's what most people would have done—but you also assumed that responsibility. I remember hearing Willie tell you once during that terrible year of Paula's illness: "If we have to take care of Paula for the rest of our lives, we will do it."

Willie also accepts life with all its baggage of joy and suffering. He's had to face greater pain than mine.

You told me during that year you were apart from your husband, you felt he wasn't sharing your pain, that he didn't understand the magnitude of your loss.

I was obsessed about Paula, and blocked out anything that could make me happy. But Willie stood by me like a rock. In Spain, when he suspected that Paula would never recover but no one had yet dared tell me that, he began to prepare me for the bad news. He was ready to bear the responsibility of Paula to the end. I never heard him complain. How could I not love that man?

He has had very serious problems of his own.

Many. Worst of all was his daughter's disappearance. You already know that Jennifer's life was a hell from the time she was a teenager, because of drugs. The police suppose she met a violent death; she may have been murdered, or may have died of an overdose and her body simply disposed of somewhere. We never found it.

And she left a baby only a few months old, Sabrina, the miracle child who was born with a death sentence but is still alive. Willie and you have been through so much . . . your love has been tested in fire.

I've cried on his shoulder many times, that's true. During the year of Paula's illness, I wept so much that my eyes became infected and I was afraid I would lose the sight of the left one. Willie held me, never asking questions or trying to console me; he let me pour out my sorrow until finally I fell asleep. I believe that the greatest love isn't the kind that's glorified in moments of success and triumph; great love is proved in times of grief. Months after Paula's death our roles were reversed: Willie wept for his vanished daughter and for all the sorrows accumulated over a lifetime. I don't want to give you the impression that we are sad people who live our lives slogging around in our misery. Just the opposite; fate has heaped blessings on us both. Every day, without fail, we give thanks for the blessing of having found each other, for our family, for everything we have. Comparing the good and the bad in my life, I would say that I have been very happy. I've been lucky in love; in the love of my mother and my children, and now, the love of my grandchildren. Also, in the love of a few men, and of certain friends who have been with me in my failures and successes: my friend Pía Leiva in Chile; my friend Ildemaro in Venezuela; my friend Tabra in California. When I add it all up, the twenty-eight years of happiness I had with my daughter are much more important than the eternity of her death. If I had to go back and live every painful instant of the year 1992, I would do it to have the years when Paula was healthy. I know people who have told me they will never have children because they don't want to suffer if something happens to them. Then would it be better not to be born? Because suffering is inevitable.

There's a poem by Pablo Neruda that says: "Enduring, the river destroys itself." As it flows, its waters dry up, and enduring, we ourselves are destroyed. Every instant of our enduring is an instant of destruction. Shall I refuse to take a step for fear of the consequences, or shall I accept them, even though the results are not always felicitous? With or without meaning, life must be lived. In the end, in old age, is when we most need strength and are the weakest, when we most need money and have the least, when we most require friends and are hardest hit by loneliness. If we knew at the beginning of life that we would become infirm

and lonely, we would choose to die young. Life ends on a low note, in a minor key, almost soundlessly, as we walk toward the absolute silence of death. Didn't you write: "Silence before being born, silence after death; life is nothing but noise between two unfathomable silences"?

Yes, in *Paula*, I think. In my fifty-some years of life, at the end of many abandonments, separations, sorrows, successes, pains, pleasures, joys, and laughter—because I have laughed a lot, I have to say that—I have learned to be open to any experience that comes along. I'm not afraid to suffer, or decline, grow old, have a hard time, be spoken ill of, die. I do fear violence. We suffer less if we are open to life. When we put up defenses, try to protect ourselves in any way possible, we anticipate suffering that may not come.

Have you had things in common with the men you've loved?

Nothing except intelligence. Although to be truthful, I admit I never learned whether the big-eared kid in Bolivia had any sense because we never exchanged a word. According to Tío Ramón, the only thing the head is good for is holding the ears apart.

What is the thing that first attracts you?

When I was young, it was the interest the man showed in me. All he had to do was throw me a meaningful glance and I blossomed, and that made him a prince in my eyes. It was easy. Later I became a little more selective; I noticed the hands, eyes, smell, the body in general, the voice. . . . As you see, purely spiritual characteristics! Today I'm seduced by strength of character. I don't like weak people. And one thing that excites me a lot is a sense of humor. If I laugh with a man, I usually want to lead him to bed—although I don't, of course. I'm a respectable grandmother. (*She laughs provocatively.*)

That works both ways. A woman who has a capacity for laughter and a sense of humor is attractive to men. Maybe they feel she's lowering her defenses, that she doesn't take conventions

and social rules too seriously.

If that's true, then where is my line of admirers? In all my relationships I've been the circus ringmaster, the one who organizes the spectacle, the excitement, the game. When I was married to Miguel, I went so far as to start a theater company made up of our friends; the show was nearly professional. I wore costumes, planned exotic meals, covered myself in feathers, and danced on the table if circumstances required it.

You're speaking in the past tense.

I can't do that kind of cartwheels for a man any longer. Only for my grandchildren now.

How do you define strength of character?

A certain stoicism and generosity, not complaining, setting goals and meeting them, having an optimistic vision of life, flexibility, accepting one's fate boldly, recognizing mistakes and correcting them. I'm also attracted to people who dare to be different.

There are many instances, not only in literature but real life, of insecure women who think they won't be loved the way they give love, women who are terrified of being abandoned.

I don't keep track of such things—they're boring. How much I'm loved has nothing to do with how much I love. I love my grandchildren and my children much more than they love me. Why does that matter?

But with your companion, your lover, it isn't the same thing.

I've been lucky, they've loved me enough. That gives me confidence not to keep a running tab. What matters to me is what I offer; how it's received is no longer my problem.

Well, then, let's talk about love at its fullest. What are the most memorable moments you've experienced? Give me an anecdote.

Erotica? I don't know, my memories all blend together. (*It is obvious she is enjoying herself.*)

There were so many?

No, not that many, but I have a bad memory. (*Roguishly*)

We'll go back to your books, if you prefer. Which of the couples I've come to know so well represent the most torrid love?

Irene and Francisco in *Of Love and Shadows*. They loved with passion and tenderness; they were supportive of each other, they shared emotions and ideals. For a love like that I would leave everything I have in this world! Except my grandchildren, of course.

But in that book, too, the lack of communication between Irene and her mother is notable. How do you think understanding, harmony, and good communication with one's grandchildren is best achieved?

You ask such difficult questions! What authority do I have to answer that? I've committed every mistake possible. But common sense says that the combination of love, clear boundaries, and frankness works well. My children didn't have problems, not even in adolescence. Miguel imposed the rule of respect in the house—that helped a lot; we weren't a family that went around slamming doors or insulting each other. We treated our children as if they were dwarves: short adults. A system of mutual loyalties developed, based on respect. The family knows that my loyalty to them is unconditional; whatever happens, whatever they do, I will always be there to stand by them and help them.

And they for you?

How can I know that? I hope that when the shoe is on the other foot, they'll return the favor, but I would like to think that will never happen; I've already told you I'm not good at receiving. Don't you hate to depend on others, to ask for help, even from your children?

I don't want to even think about it. The other day you mentioned an episode in Nicolás's teen years; to avoid having to go to school, he took some tranquilizers he found in the house, and nearly died.

That happened soon after I returned from the unfortunate melodrama with my lover in Spain, in 1978. The children suffered a great deal in my absence. Nicolás had a series of accidents; it was as if he was trying to attract attention by hurting himself. Once he dived into the river and split his head on a rock; he nearly died then, too. Another time he jumped from a tower at school and broke an arm. When Paula had two wisdom teeth pulled, they prescribed Valium to keep her calm. Nicolás saw that his sister wasn't going to school and thought that if he took the same medication he could stay home, too. He swallowed a pill, felt no effect, took another—nothing—then kept taking them until he emptied the vial. They were close to operating, thinking he must have a cerebral hematoma resulting from a fall; luckily, two days later, Nicolás woke up and quickly recovered. I don't think he meant to kill himself, but subconsciously he may have wanted to punish me for having abandoned him. Now, as adults, we have talked all that out calmly. Every time we do, I slap his cheeks for being so dumb.

I can't forget that Nicolás used a slingshot to fire eggs from his window onto the building next door. In that Caracas heat, I imagine they became instant omelets. And you say your children never had problems?

(On the defensive.) Not the kinds of problems that crush other parents: they were polite, calm, good students, independent, affectionate, happy, friendly. They didn't run with a bad crowd, they didn't take drugs, they never drank . . . they didn't even smoke.

**There aren't any children like that anymore. Was Nicolás closer
to you than Paula at the time you went off to Spain?**

He was three years younger and more vulnerable than Paula, but
I think both were equally dependent.

How did Paula react to those same events?

When I left, she turned into a little sergeant; she took on total
responsibility of the house, the family, and her brother. She got excel-
lent grades, and took French and music classes; it was as if she wanted to wear herself out. Our relationship was somewhat strained when
I came back, as is only logical. For some years, neither of my children wanted to talk about it. When they were ready to go to college,
we sat down one day and had a serious talk—we hashed it all out.

**Do you think that their love was stronger than their disap-
proval—if they did disapprove? That everyday relations were
tarnished but not their love?**

After Paula died, Ernesto, her husband, handed me a box filled
with their love letters. Take it, he said, I want you to know a different side of your daughter's character and life. For one year, early in
their relationship, they had to be apart because she was studying in
Virginia and he had a job in Madrid. They wrote each other every
day, sometimes two and three letters within a few hours, a passionate correspondence written in all sorts of places: in buses, classes,
waiting rooms, outdoors, bed. Ernesto had the incredible generosity
to share that blessed box with me. In her letters, Paula was not only
revealed as a very passionate woman, but she also told her version of
the family and the past. She wrote Ernesto about a happy childhood
and a relationship with me as marvelous as the one I have with my
mother. That was the most extraordinary gift I have ever received,
the greatest consolation during all that period of pain. I learned that
I had been a better mother than I had suspected. I had always borne
the guilt of having taken my children from Chile against their will,
of having separated them from their grandparents, whom they

adored, from their home, their friends, their school, their neighborhood, everything familiar to them, and taken them to an unknown future. And then I abandoned them for a brief period. I saw myself as an unstable woman, dissatisfied, filled with fantasies. I wasn't your typical mother. When they were little, I dressed like a hippie and drove a car painted with flowers; I think my children were horrified by such excesses. Even so, in her letters to Ernesto, Paula remembered that time with great sympathy and love.

You say that on the one hand your children were amused by your eccentricity and your love of the extravagant, but, on the other hand, they felt they stood out. How did you reconcile motherhood with feminism when you were young?

I don't know. Stumbling along, I guess, improvising, sometimes badly, sometimes a little better. I never questioned motherhood; feminism had nothing to do with my role as a mother. Feminism questioned everything else: my relationship with men, with society, with laws, with sexuality, with fashion, with my job, with money, and so on, but to me, motherhood was something as taken for granted and as natural as breathing. I never considered not having children, and when they were born, something basic changed in me forever. I ceased to be an individual and became part of an indivisible trio.

Don't you think that in the case of your grandchildren, you still have a tendency to make the decisions and feel you are the one person responsible for them?

Yes, but I'm going through analysis about that, and before long, let's say twenty or thirty years, I will be cured. (*She laughs.*)

How does that tendency manifest itself currently?

Ever since Nicolás and Celia got divorced, I feel as if I'm the children's mother. But don't worry, I'll get over it. That's what I keep telling them; let's see if they calm down, poor things.

You wore out your pen writing your mother, your friends, the

parents of your friends. You write Pía Leiva in Chile several times a week, a friend you haven't seen for almost twenty years, back to the time you were living in Venezuela. If you were forbidden to write, could you live?

It's hard for me to imagine life without the written word and the friendship of letters. I love the mail, the stamped letter in its envelope. There's nothing comparable to that handwritten letter that has traveled to my doorstep. I open it and hear the voice of the person who wrote it, as clear as a bell. From the handwriting, I can judge the sender's state of mind. That's why my mother and I write the old-fashioned way, and fall back on the fax and e-mail only for emergencies. There is something private, inviolable, intimate in a letter, that modern methods don't have. The idea that Tío Ramón can read a fax inhibits my mother and me. She has an expression to describe that necessary prudence: buttoning your lip. What I most appreciate in my mother is her viperous tongue, her devastating sarcasm, her perverse sense of observation, her delicious jokes. With her lip buttoned, my mother becomes an insipid great-grandmother.

Muses, Angels, and Demons

You talk about writing as if you were a medium.

I often feel that I am. I can control form, but not content. I begin to tell a story and have no idea where I am going; the characters take over, and sometimes the book ends in a way I hadn't expected. It's as if the story and characters existed in another dimension, and by some stroke of fate, I am in sync with them.

Like magic?

Someone suggested to me that I try automatic writing—just let my hand go while I'm in a state of trance—but I haven't tried it yet.

Have you been hypnotized?

They've tried, but I can't relax, and I end up hypnotizing the hypnotizer. (*Completely serious*)

Was there ever a writer in your family? Weren't some of the Barros Moreira writers?

One of my great-grandfathers wrote poetry, and my Uncle Marcos wrote a book when he was young.

Which ended up in the cellar because your grandfather confiscated it.

Let's just say that it didn't sell and that's why it ended up in the cellar. I've been told that it was rather good.

What was it about?

About my uncle's spiritual transformation in India.

I see a tendency toward mysticism in your family. The most recent seems to be your brother Juan, a professor of political science, a Marxist and atheist who took up theology.

After three years of exploring the mysteries of God, he realized he had no calling and now is back teaching political science. He's too honest not to listen to his own doubts. My brother is a wise man, and I love him very much, but sometimes I want to shake him like a mop, to see if I can shake some scruples out of him, for God's sake. It's true what you say about mysticism in my family. My Uncle Marcos has dedicated his life to spiritual practices. When he was young, he went to India seeking illumination, and returned nothing but skin and bones, dressed like a fakir and eating carrots. He's over seventy now, and a well-respected guru. My grandmother was a spiritist, and my aunt Teresa was a saint; she grew the stubs of wings on her shoulders. My mother is very religious. All my grandmother's family, the Barros Moreira, were slightly mystical; I guess that contributed to their reputation for being a little "touched."

You say you begin to write without a defined plan—except in the case of *Of Love and Shadows,* which was a conscious act of denunciation. Was there one author who influenced you more than any other?

My life has been influenced by European and North American feminists, who shaped my personality, but in literature nearly all the figures were male. Gabriel García Márquez gave me the freedom to let my imagination fly; José Donoso, to dig into family secrets; Mario Vargas Llosa, to use the tricks of journalism; Pablo Neruda, to describe nature and explore the world of the senses. Other great Latin American authors, like Ernesto Sábato, Julio Cortázar, Jorge Luis Borges, Juan Rulfo, Carlos Fuentes, and Octavio Paz, paved the way for me. My childhood reading also left its mark: the brothers Salgari, Verne, London, Stevenson, Defoe, Wilde, Shaw, Twain, and many others. They gave me a taste for drama, strong characters, adventure, and ringing plots; I detest minimalist literature. And then Shakespeare, whom I read at the age of nine for the same reason that other people watch soap operas—to pry into other's lives.

And sensuality?

I got that as a teenager from secret readings of *The Thousand and One Nights* and similar books. Later I looked for it in Neruda, the poet of the senses. There is no one like Neruda for describing an aroma, a color, a sound.

If for you Neruda was a poet of the senses, what do you owe to Gabriela Mistral?

I knew very little about her work because I wasn't educated in Chile and didn't read her when I was young. But something strange happened to me in Cuba, where I was asked to record her poems. I had to rehearse for several days, reading aloud, over and over. . . . As I read, I found I was feeling the tremendous weight of Gabriela Mistral. Some of her more sentimental lines, like, *oh, little baby feet, blue with cold, Dear God, how can they see you and not cover you,* slipped from my mind, but her extraordinary spiritual voice swept into my life like a hurricane. She was a somber woman . . . she revealed herself to me.

If you leave her poetry behind and consider her many epistolary literary and journal pieces, you find that she's known around the world. You have in common with her your gypsy life, your residence in foreign lands, and your interest in social causes.

Going back to literary influences, I should acknowledge the Russian writers I read so passionately: Dostoyevski, Tolstoy, Chekhov—as well as science fiction. There is a philosophical aspect in good science fiction that strongly attracts me—for example, speculations on time that remind me of Borges.

Strangely enough, science fiction and magical realism have a lot of elements in common: the double, space travel, parallel lives, transmutation of a human into another creature—Cortázar's *axolotl* comes to mind—but the difference is that magical realism sometimes moves into the metaphysical, questions time with modulations that can be lyrical. Do you play with time in any of your works?

No. Except in the circular form of narrating I often find myself trapped in. I feel that everything occurs simultaneously, or that everything is inescapably repeated. For me, this isn't a literary technique. I have the same sensation in real life—that the time of calendars and clocks is a convention we accept in order to understand reality, but that there is no past, present, or future; everything *exists*, eternally. Everything that happened, that will happen, that occurs in this moment, is part of reality. In literature, memory and words work the miracle of erasing the convention of time.

In *Paula*, based on the pain of your daughter's death, you stop time; you set the narrative in a kind of sustained time, as if it were a myth, an action repeated within itself. You also used that technique in the story "Walimai."

Well, I think in *The House of the Spirits*, too.

In which part?

When Clara dies. Also, after Alba is tortured, and she thinks she is dying, the ghost of her grandmother appears, takes her in her arms, and tells her that grace is not dying, grace is living.

And also when Férula dies. In those moments you postulate something metaphysical, Borgesian, but in your work that phenomenon always seems connected with love: a mother's love, love between a man and a woman, sisterly love.

Love—and at times sorrow—allow us to penetrate the veil that separates the apparently real from the spiritual, and connect us with other dimensions. That is clear in my relationship with Paula. Our communication is permanent, profound; it is as if she lived in me and I died in her. I do not, however, expect to see her ghost on the stairway, as some say they see her in my house.

You know that last night I slept in the room where Paula died. I was awakened at midnight by a delicious aroma of fresh flowers . . . jasmine, maybe.

Those were her favorite flowers. It's possible that the perfume drifted up from the garden.

It isn't the season for jasmine.

I don't feel I'm separated from the dead I have loved. My grandmother died nearly fifty years ago, but she is still a real presence for me. I have her photograph on my work table; I look into her eyes and feel the connection, just as I do with my grandfather, my mother-in-law, Paulita, and others. If I have spiritual doubts, I think about my grandmother. If I have to face a new challenge, my grandfather comes to give me courage; if I have to resolve a family problem, it is always the ghost of Miguel's mother, Granny, I see. Paula, while still a child, ended up taking care of her. Her gesture of hiding her Granny's empty bottles to spare her the humiliation of having others learn she was drinking secretly says more about Paula than any words can do. Granny was an angel who had lost her way in this world. When I ask her ghost what I must do, I seem to see her sky-blue eyes and her smile. She opens her arms to me and approves everything; she doesn't judge, she doesn't condemn. If it's a problem connected with my work, with creativity, with organization, with a character, Paula comes to my aid, because that's what she did in life. I would pick up the telephone and she always had an original angle; she was a psychologist and a teacher. Her favorite answer to my practical questions was, "What is the most generous thing you can do in this case, Mama?"

Was Granny still living when you and Miguel separated?

No. She died the day we decided to separate the first time. Later we reconciled, and lived together nine more years.

You sometimes talk about your "demons." What are you referring to?

Obsessions we all have and which, inevitably, live in the pages I write. Sometimes I am specifically referring to the demon of my childhood. Remember that when I was a girl, the Catholic church still taught that the devil existed. The nuns threatened me with the tortures of hell, but today no one talks about those things. Satan is definitely out of style. The rituals have also changed; the Latin mass and priestly garb are things of the past; today, priests go around in blue jeans and nuns wear lipstick. In a way, I regret it, because if they take away our colorful demons and regal ceremonies, there won't be as many writers. Nothing better than a childhood peopled with terrors to spur imagination.

Your family was Catholic, but you have said that when you were fifteen you left religion forever. I imagine that wasn't an easy decision.

It was inevitable, but that hasn't kept my own spirituality from developing over the years. My grandfather had what he called "a coal-miner's faith"—that is, he practiced religion without asking the questions that might weaken his beliefs. But he also accommodated religion to his needs. He went to communion every Sunday, but he never confessed because he didn't trust the priests. He believed in miracles, but he mocked the saints and said he didn't have to read the Bible because if he did, he would end up an atheist. Even so, the two books that were always at hand in the last years of his long old age were the Bible and the Encyclopedia Britannica.

The spiritual components of your work have often been pointed out. Aside from Catholicism, is there another religion that attracts you?

Catholicism doesn't attract me; neither do other religions. But I've discovered that the more gods a religion has, the more tolerant it is. The worst crimes against humanity have been committed in the name of a unique god. Buddhism would be appealing to me if it weren't so male-oriented—like all traditional religions.

Pentecostal and charismatic movements have swept across Latin America with devastating force.

They offer a direct experience of the divine: the trance. For that same reason, in the large cities of Brazil, *candomblé, macumba,* and *umbanda*—African religions carried by the ten million black slaves brought to this country—have come out of the poor barrios and made their way into the white middle class. These religions leapfrog bureaucracy and allow the faithful to feel that divinity resides in their own bodies. This experience terrifies the hierarchies of traditional churches, which encourage fanaticism but detest mystics because they can't control them. In Brazil, I spoke about all these things with Leonardo Boff, one of the founders of liberation theology. He defined *candomblé* as an echo of the unbounded word of God. God has a thousand faces, and no one holds a monopoly on his grace. The Judeo-Christian culture is victim of the tribalist myth of the chosen people, a myth that excludes all others. *Candomblé*, and in a certain way the Pentecostals as well, maintain that the divine breath is everywhere; no one possesses or interprets it. There are no intermediaries; no one speaks *about* God but, rather, *with* God. These are lively, minimally structured movements. Religion cannot be preached or explained, it's practiced. While theologians create theories, these people fall into trances.

Have you experienced that trance you're speaking of?

No. It's an experience I envy. But I should make clear that I don't identify with *candomblé* or any similar, that is, basically fatalistic religion in which everything that happens is the will of some god and nothing can be changed. I feel closer to liberation theology, which aspires to justice. Christ is for the poor; he is a revolutionary.

Have your experiences in India changed you?

I can't deny that there's a spiritual component that distinguishes those trips from all the others I've taken. In places like India or

Nepal, my convictions waver because the laws of logic no longer function and you are forced to revise your beliefs and habits. Work, punctuality, efficiency, order—all these things lose their urgency and you begin to feel an inner silence, a respect for nature, an unjudgmental acceptance of others, and a silent appreciation for what you have, desiring nothing more. You learn that peace is the nearest thing to happiness. In Nepal, I sat down in the market to talk with an old woman who was making necklaces from tiny painted glass beads. In sign language, we told each other about our lives, showed each other our scars—hers from many falls and cuts, mine from a caesarean delivery—and we laughed with our arms about each other. In other times and in a different place, I would have taken notes in order to write a story or an article—you have to capitalize on everything—but in that market in Katmandu, the only thing that was important was a deep sense of sisterhood with that woman.

In your travels, you find muses, angels, and demons that later appear in your pages. India has marked you. I don't know whether I could bear the spectacle of such misery without feeling guilty and trying to redress it in my own way.

Ninety percent of humanity lives in poverty. We are a handful of privileged beings who consume most of the world's natural resources. In India, everything happens in the street; the concept of privacy doesn't exist. In the street, millions of human beings are born, reproduce, conduct business, suffer, and die. The natural cycles of life and death are exposed to any eyes that want to see. In India, manual labor is so cheap that a middle-class family has a dozen servants and the rich have a hundred. In the hotels there are more employees than guests. Everything is done by hand, just as it was two thousand years ago—from agriculture, where the land is still turned with a blade and a buffalo, to public administration, where carbon paper and three copies are still the rule. And that is how it must be, because nearly a billion inhabitants must be employed, even if in the most menial jobs. The comparison is inevitable. What would my destiny have been had I been born there? The contrasts are painful, but that blend of suffering, resignation, natural happiness, and beauty is very stimulating to inspiration.

Writing for the World

"Mai, tell me a story."

Mai is the affectionate name Alejandro invented for Isabel when he was learning to talk.

"Do you want a story about pirates?"

"No, about Santa Claus."

"Once upon a time," begins the young, attractive grandmother, "there was a horrid old man with horns and a devil face who peeked in windows at night, and if the children were poor, he didn't bring them any gifts—gifts were just for rich little boys and girls. . . ."

This has come out as one long thread, without a breath. Alejandro is trapped between confusion and amusement. He was expecting to hear the story of a jovial, good-natured old man who skims over the snow in a sleigh pulled by nine reindeer—with Rudolph, he of the red nose, in the lead—making sleigh bells ring. Unaware, his grandmother is telling him the story of a popular Polish legend in which the alter ego of St. Nicholas is a devilish figure sometimes known as Krupus.

But Mai isn't your ordinary grandmother. Her three grandchildren already know that she likes to change everything around. Mai's stories aren't like the ones they read in school, but they're more entertaining. This grandmother always comes out with something different, and doesn't object when the children incorporate their own versions into familiar tales. Although she is a writer who can be read by several generations of a family without a single blush, that doesn't change the fact that various religious and conservative groups have tried to ban some of her books for being obscene.

This modern Scheherazade has invented herself by telling stories, putting aside conformism and false traditions. Telling stories has saved her from poverty, from boredom, and from the greatest pain life can afford: the death of her daughter Paula.

Isabel has become a legend. Her books are sold in all the countries of the West, and there are also translations in China, Vietnam, and Korea. She is read in Russia, where her work is considered the patrimony of humanity—meaning she receives no royalties from countries once behind the Iron Curtain.

Because of her interest in education, she has created the Isabel Allende Foundation to promote the causes of the oppressed, of women, of single mothers, and of abandoned children. Whether for educational or social causes, when Isabel Allende appears to give a lecture, halls are filled to capacity. A large public eagerly awaits her. In some cases, her readers travel more than three hundred miles to see her in person. Some believe that in the United States, Isabel is read primarily by Hispanics; however, it is obvious that she has equal readership among an Anglo public. She's read by university students, chosen by professors and university curriculum committees who pay attention to the contemporary literature of Latin America. She is read by travel agents, university presidents and chancellors, by women in service clubs, restaurant waitresses, traveling salesmen, intellectuals, and anyone who wants an entertaining book to lighten the hours of a long trip. Isabel Allende is read by cultivated, erudite, and demanding readers, as well as people who want to spend a few entertaining hours in escape from reality.

If you go to Mexico and walk through the streets there, you will see the covers of Isabel's books on Insurgentes Avenue; if you go to Buenos Aires, you will see them in the bookstores on Calle Florida; if you find yourself in Madrid, they're on the Gran Vía; in France, Italy, Germany, and Portugal, Isabel Allende's books are prominently displayed. The jackets vary by edition and language, some done by great artists and others by unknown artists. The author herself has lost track of how many there are. She knows only that in Germany, in recent years, nearly three million copies of *The House of the Spirits* have been sold. In all, it is calculated that sales of Isabel Allende's books have surpassed thirty million copies, not counting the pirated editions that appear in many countries as well as in the Communist world in the U-Bahn in Frankfurt, the piazzas of Italy, and the streets of Chile. And in January 2000, in a nine-day period and in Italy alone, 350,000 copies of *Daughter of Fortune* were sold. Not just the Western world, the entire world reads Isabel Allende.

Critics, particularly Chilean critics, Isabel's countrymen, are sometimes puzzled by the success of an author who, according to them, is a García Márquez epigone, simply a second-rank writer, when Chilean authors well known both inside and outside the country have yet to receive the same international recognition. "No one is a prophet in her own land," Isabel always says when that is mentioned. Some read her to criticize her; others to enjoy her. All that ever reaches her, she says with the humor that characterizes her work, are love letters, so she's never aware of those who don't like her books. Only people who like her a lot take the trouble to write.

The office responsible for managing Isabel's relations with her readers and for mailing the replies she answers by hand, keeps an archive of articles published about her books around the world. These articles come from two sources: journalists and academicians. Academicians's comments are not always favorable; the journalists' pieces range from panegyric and effusive elegy to accusations of excessively sentimental elements in her work. Everything appears in the critiques: from classifying her writing as bordering on romance with fantastic components sprinkled on indiscriminately, or as literature verging on soap opera, to applauding her work for its force, its fantasy, its thematic variety, its political consciousness, its social criticism, its love and unfailing humor.

Master's and doctoral theses have been written on Isabel's work, not just in the United States, but in Canada and all of Europe and Latin America. Hundreds of specialized studies on Isabel Allende are catalogued in North American universities. Between March and June of 2000, at Stanford University in California, eight new studies on her work were added to the bibliography. At the prestigious Yale University, the respected Hispanist Manuel Durán directed a thesis on feminism in Isabel's novels. McGill University in Canada has approved a thesis on the novelistic language of our Chilean author, and the University of Perpignan in France has dedicated a critical study to her, the result of a collaboration among several specialists in Spanish American literature. At the beginning of her novelistic career, Isabel wrote with good humor about the seriousness of critical studies by universities: "[L]ike most normal human beings, I had never read a page of criticism, and could not have imagined that books are analyzed in universities with the same intensity accorded stars in the firmament."

Isabel, who never studied literature, and who does not participate in literary conferences or workshops, acknowledges that she discovered the structure of *Eva Luna* only after reading her critics. In Barcelona, at a party given by her literary agent, Carmen Balcells, following the publication of *The House of the Spirits,* Isabel found herself face to face for the first time with a literary critic. "I still remember the first question I was asked in an interview conducted by the most renowned literary critic of the moment: 'Can you explain the cyclical structure of your novel?' My expression must have been totally bovine, I hadn't any idea what he was talking about. In my vocabulary, only buildings had 'structure,' and the only 'cyclical' I was familiar with referred to the moon or menstruation."

If as a child she hid behind a book, we can also imagine that because of her size and fine features, she must have seemed like a lost little girl who ended up in the wrong grade. There are photographs from that period that testify to how solemn she was. "She could be very serious," says Cecilia Viel, a childhood friend in Chile, "but she was also funny and quick." Isabel is like her books: laughter, tears, meditations, love, turbulence.

Readers and students familiarly call her Isabel; they write her, call her, send her their articles, and think of themselves as her friends. When she gives lectures at North American universities, she willingly signs books, so many that she sometimes spends hours writing inscriptions, always adding a forget-me-not—her personal sign—traced with a single stroke of her pen. Her fans don't stop with only one of her books, they read many; she is grateful that they ask for her autograph, buy her books, and, as she herself says with amazement, "still read me . . . how long will such loyalty last?" With stacks of books in their arms, her admirers wait patiently in line. Many bring her gifts, letters, poems. Isabel, in a trademark fringed shawl, takes her time. When someone needs special attention, she gives it as if the person were her one friend in the world. The lights in the hall are gradually turned off as the despairing custodian looks at his watch and sighs.

Success

How did you react when you became famous? For someone whose aspiration was to have a husband and children, a working woman whose best friend is her mother, a person with her feet planted on the ground, it must have been difficult to accept the fame that came so suddenly.

It didn't come suddenly, Celia; it was gradual. I had no sense of the impact of *The House of the Spirits* until several years later. I was living in Venezuela, where no one talked about the book, which had been published in Europe. It was several years before it was published in Latin America, and it had very little impact in Venezuela. I had begun to receive invitations from the United States, and made several publicity tours in Europe before I had the least recognition in my own part of the world.

The instantaneous spotlight was Europe, and from there it shifted to the United States?

From Europe, that book moved slowly to Latin America, then was published in the States. But in Spanish departments in North American universities, they were already talking about the book; that's why I received the invitations.

Before anyone knew the book in Venezuela, Chile, Argentina, or Mexico, you were being read in German and Swedish, which explains why your detractors called you a marginal and trans-

gressing writer.

(*Isabel laughs heartily and keeps talking as if she hadn't heard any-thing.*) My relationship with my European editors is one of great loy-alty; it has lasted longer than most of my marriages.

When did the book come out in English?

Four years after publication in Spain.

I thought it had been almost simultaneous.

Magda Bogin did that translation for Knopf. All my other books have been translated by Margaret Sayers Peden.

Do you think translation into English was decisive?

The greatest determining factor was the success in Europe; that opened doors in the United States. But I knew almost nothing of that where I was living in Caracas. No one knew me or asked me to sign a book; that happened much later, when *Of Love and Shadows* had already been published and I was about to begin *Eva Luna*. Once I saw a man with one of my novels under his arm and I ran up and said, "That's my book!" "No," he replied, "it's mine, I bought it." "Do you want me to sign it?" I persisted. "No!" he said quite angrily.

You had two books published in several languages yet you kept working twelve hours a day at a school? (*She is not surprised at my amazement.*) **I suppose you were still writing at night before going to bed.**

I didn't dare leave a secure job to pursue a wild literary adven-ture. I didn't feel as if I was a writer. I thought I'd had the incredible luck to hit the target a couple of times, but that it wouldn't happen again. Remember, I was an immigrant; security was important to our family. I'd come to Venezuela in 1975 with nothing—no friends, no documents, no work, no money. A steady job was essential. I had invested a lot of my life in the school; I had stock, it was my future.

How do you react to the throngs of known and unknown people who read you throughout the world? Do their opinions concern you?

People who come up to me, or write me, normally like my work, but there must be many who detest my books and just don't go to the trouble of telling me. When I get those marvelous, flattering letters you've seen, I always keep in mind the people who have a different opinion. But how could I help but be moved by the generous readers who do write me? Some tell me about their lives, share their intimate thoughts with me, their memories, their sorrows.

You weren't like that when I met you. You've become more spiritual since Paula's death. You have acquired a special power; you have a beneficent effect on people. You seem to maintain an air of calm, of inner equilibrium, even in the kinds of situations that put us to the test. Is it resignation? Fatalism?

According to Buddhists, birth and death are inscribed in the Book of Destiny. My grandfather said the same thing in his own way; there's no point of running inside the train. Our way is written; it has its direction and velocity—we can't hurry it along. No matter how hard we run inside the train, we get where we're going at exactly the same time.

Let's talk about adulation. Celebrities often become a little paranoid; they begin to think they're being called and sought after only to be taken advantage of. They escape, they hide behind locked doors, because they find people clinging to them, hounding them. How come you haven't become cautious? How do you distinguish adulation from a sincere compliment?

I love compliments, but my family doesn't let them go to my head. The minute I get a little full of myself, they give me a yank and I fall flat on my face. My grandchildren are merciless. Willie and my assistants help me protect my privacy. My office is like a Chinese screen that isolates me from everything. I confess that to a certain degree, I *have* become a little paranoid, because I get endless requests: money, books, favors—will I write a prologue, serve on a jury, talk, write, and on and on. Perfect strangers get furious because I won't help them buy a taxi, or because I don't have time to edit a six-hundred-page manuscript written by their dear old mother, may she rest in peace. I have to say no to ninety-five percent of the invitations I get, and put the rest through a screening process. I honor requests; I put part of my income into helping others, but I have that already set up: education, women's subjects, AIDS. I don't participate actively in politics. The correspondence that comes to me from the kind readers makes up for all the rest. I answer those letters with great emotion, grateful for the enormous good fortune of knowing that my books have touched the lives of others.

Not all writers react in the same way. They would think that answering letters by hand is a waste of time, or just plain stupid.

So they tell me . . . but I can't stop doing it. The letters I get are moving, enthusiastic, sometimes intimate, as if the writer and I had known each other all our lives. How could I not answer them?

Considering the sales figures and the wide distribution of your books, you don't really have to spend hours signing books in a bookstore, for example.

I don't do signings to sell books, but to be in contact with my readers. Some wait in line for hours for an autograph—at least I'm sitting down—and they bring piles of well-thumbed books.

Your audiences swell when you sign books. I know that some of your readers invest hours to come see you. The prime example was in Puerto Rico. You were supposed to sign from three to four-thirty, but it was Saturday; the word got around the central business district where the bookstore was located, and the line kept growing until it spilled into the parking lot.

By six my hand was cramped; they brought me a pail of hot salt-water so I could soak it a while, and I kept signing to eight-thirty. By the end, my name looked like a squashed tick.

In your books you establish a personal contact with each reader; you create a close, intimate, friendly space. Maybe when you appear in person, you give that same impression of intimacy, and that's why people want to come back again and again to see you. It's amazing that their enthusiasm is so enduring. You came out with your first novel in 1982, and you're still hot. Julio Iglesias created a furor in that same period, and now almost no one listens to him. The United States is a country given to fads. Think about it, how long does a fad last in this country?

Who told you no one listens to Julio Iglesias anymore? I know women who still faint when he moans. As for my books being hot in the United States, that's recent. The greatest impact has been in Europe and Latin America. My books sell well in the U.S., and are still in print, but my real success here began with *Paula*.

In 1993 you began to publish with HarperCollins. This phase clearly put you on the list of Latin American writers living in the United States. A rather short list. What was the first book you published with them?

The Infinite Plan, which had been published in Spain the year before. When the translation came out in the United States, Paula had just died and I had to go on a publicity tour.

The most upsetting thing for a woman of action is the paralysis and confusion resulting from sorrow.

It's true. I felt as if I were wearing armor that separated me from the world, but I kept working like an automaton, and I think that helped me a lot. I had to travel to eighteen cities in the U.S., dragging a suitcase and my soul. (*A veil of sadness falls over her.*)

How were you received? Did people know about your tragedy? Tell me about those days.

The place where I was reading was always filled, and the audience very enthusiastic, although most didn't know that my daughter had recently died.

Did the attention and applause of all those strangers ease your sorrow?

Of course. There would be an invigorating energy that was like a current of optimism, sometimes humor. But afterward I had to go back alone to a hotel room or a plane, and then sadness hit me like a ton of bricks.

Do you feel that you have a well-informed audience?

Usually, the people who come to hear a writer know something about her work; if they didn't, they wouldn't come. Let's say that at those times I have a patient . . . and captive . . . audience. They're trapped in their seats, poor things. Who can dare leave the room under the beady eye of the speaker? But let's not lose perspective; the fact that an auditorium is filled doesn't mean I have the world at my feet, only that there are still people who read in this world, and people who want to hear a story. "Once upon a time. . . ." Oh, the insatiable appetite we humans have for stories!

How long do you think your fame and your best-sellers will last?

Who can know that? According to my mother's tarot cards, my books should have disappeared from sight some time ago. I don't think about it because it scares me to death. One day my books will stop selling, and I will be an anonymous old woman. I've had success, sorrow, love, travel, imaginings. . . . To be truthful, I've lived about four lives.

Your agent, Carmen Balcells, divides your career between what

you did before *Paula,* and what is still to come. She says the previous six books form a block and that with *Paula* you begin a new phase.

Carmen never loses hope that I will grow up and flower. She's been waiting fifteen years.

Let's talk about new women writers. You got me started reading several women writers whom you've given—and are still giving— a little boost. Not all writers do that. The literary world is rife with rivalries, jealousy, envy, sharp elbows, dirty punches . . . it's a rather ugly club. It seems you have to step on others to get ahead.

There's more than enough room for everyone in literature. In fact, half the people around me are writing a novel, and I know several teenagers who are already deep into their memoirs. You know how I see it? We writers are explorers slashing a trail through the jungle with our machetes. If we work together, we can build a road, and all of us will move forward with glory and majesty. That doesn't mean that I'm able to write prologues and read the hundreds of manuscripts that end up on my desk. But if we start tripping and hacking at each other, the jungle will eat us alive. The larger the team opening the path for literature, the more readers we'll have. Every reader who gets hooked on one of my books will later look for other Latin American writers. The numbers of stories are infinite. Words are free, and people's need to be told stories is limitless. Why go around playing dirty tricks?

That was how Julio Cortázar was. He put me in contact with other writers, and recommended books to me. If you needed information, he'd say, "Write so and so." He was extremely helpful. Another generous man was Eduardo Gudiño Kieffer, the Argentine writer, who gave me a full list of the best Argentine women writers. Did you know Marta Lynch?

I've read her, and I saw her once, shortly before she died.

Gudiño Kieffer told me that I looked like Marta Lynch, and dressed like her. When I met her, I didn't see the resemblance, but I was flattered nonetheless. Like you, he told me that "in the sea of literature there are lots of fish that know how to swim, and there's room for all of them." Even so, no one else wanted to give me the names of women writers. But he took the time to find their addresses and phone numbers. In those days, the only women in anthologies were Sor Juana Inés de la Cruz and Gabriela Mistral. I hope your own generosity doesn't take over your life. You won't have a moment of peace.

We have to change our telephone number every year because the phone rings constantly—it drives us crazy. This Christmas we had people in sleeping bags, like tramps, even after we rented a few rooms in a nearby bed-and-breakfast.

Do you like having a houseful of people?

As long as it isn't for too long a time. When everyone finally left in January, and we were alone, Willie stripped off all his clothes and ran outside jumping and whooping like a demented Tarzan recapturing invaded territory.

A woman once told me she couldn't knit around her husband because he felt she was ignoring him. The poor woman had to make up the story that she was doing it for her arthritis, under doctor's orders. If just knitting can be that complicated, you obviously need a private place where you can write. Does it bother Willie when you shut the door and work? What is your schedule?

The truth is that I've never asked him if it bothers him. I think he likes to see me busy; that way, I'm not at him to change the paintings or move the furniture. We keep strict schedules. We get up very early. Willie goes off to work, and I walk for an hour; then I go to my little study, which is a coach house at the back of the house near Willie's office. Sometimes we have a cup of coffee, or eat lunch together, and about five we're back in the house. We cook together, look after the grandchildren. There's always something to do.

Your mother thought you would be an actress; your women friends would have sworn you'd be a painter. Winston Churchill won the Nobel Prize for literature and was respected as a painter. Will that be true of you?

What in the world are you saying? Occasionally, I paint something or other, with much more bravura than talent. That doesn't make me an artist. I also tend to run downstairs, but I couldn't compete as an athlete, Celia. It relaxes me to work with my hands; that's why I have a room filled with papers, paints, cloth scraps, and all the things I use for crafts. But if I had to work with my hands, I'd make empanadas, which would be more practical. (*The more she laughs, the more I study a couple of her paintings on the wall, which aren't at all bad.*)

I've been told that you make every one of the cards you use to answer your readers' letters.

It's a kind of meditation. But I don't do them all. Most are embroidered by my sister-friend Pía Leiva in Chile; she sends them to me in huge envelopes. They're so pretty that often they're stolen from the mail.

In one lecture, a member of the audience asked how you would define yourself, and without blinking an eye, you answered, "a flamboyant bitch."

"Flamboyant bitch" sounds better in English than in Spanish. The translation is very harsh: *perra flamígera*. How would you define yourself? It's a typical question but one I never know how to answer. I threw out that phrase for the fun of shocking the audience, and, as my mother always says, often when I make a joke I get in trouble. Now I'll have to explain that away till the day I die. What I wanted to say was that I have no prejudices and that I can be a showboat. Don't look at me like that! I know that goes against what we were saying earlier, that I'm very shy in social situations. That's just another of my many contradictions.

You've had a lot of praise, a lot of success. How has that changed you?

I don't think it has. I'm not terribly impressed by the success of others. I don't see why I should be when it comes to me. My life has been like a roller coaster: all ups and downs. When I'm down, I don't stay depressed, because it won't be forever, and when I'm up, I look at the precipice at my feet and feel humbled. It can all end in a few seconds.

Are you able to have a private life?

Of course. I'm not a rock star, I'm just a writer. How many people do you think read in this world? Besides, the United States is a huge country. Here I'm one of more than thirty million Latin immigrants.

Where are you most famous? Where are you least read?

I'm most famous in my own home. I'm read most in Germany, Italy, Holland, Denmark, and, of course, Spain and all the Spanish-speaking Latin American countries. I'm most often recognized in Chile, of course. Where am I least known? In the galaxy and beyond.

Today

At a writers' conference at Montclair State College shortly after the publication of *La casa de los espíritus*, when I saw Isabel dressed in a peasant skirt with an enormous leather briefcase in hand, wearing a kind of gray poncho or ruana to top off her outfit, her face bare of makeup, she had the frightened expression of a little girl who had been set down in the midst of a noisy party of total strangers. She could barely see over the lectern where she stood to address us, and read her words about the novel in a monotone. I think that Tío Ramón's saying, "Always remember that others are more afraid than you" fell a little short before the sudden onslaught of fame that accompanied her first novel, and at first it was difficult for her to absorb it all.

The Isabel of today bears no resemblance to that woman. Looking ten years younger than her age, extremely photogenic, she could pass for a professional actress when she performs in public. Her clothing has a personal flair inspired by the freedom of the sixties, but in more intense colors—she prefers all shades of red and the dramatic effect of black—and fine fabrics that fall in soft pleats and ripple as she walks. She has not lost the sense of humor that made her column "*Los impertinentes*" famous in Chile. She laughs freely at herself and her supposed weak points, and incorporates the humorous spontaneity of her grandchildren into her repertoire. Memorized jokes leave her cold; she doesn't laugh because she says she doesn't understand them. She parries journalists' questions deftly, leading them down the path of irony and humor, skillfully sorting her way through the reefs of vexatious queries.

Her fame has not gone to her head. She knows she is a privileged woman with enormous responsibilities, and Paula's death taught her an unforgettable lesson about how fleeting earthly blessings are. With fame, her visibility increased, and, along with that, following the implacable law of opposites, her personal vulnerability. She does not cling to material objects and she is generous with the money she has earned with her computer's keyboard, exploiting no one. She accepts sincere praise with gratitude, almost humility, and accepts criticism with equanimity. The lines of Rudyard Kipling describe her: *If you can meet with Triumph and Disaster and treat those impostors just the same. . . .*

Isabel Allende has lived in the city of San Rafael, north of San Francisco, since she married Willie. At least three times a week she walks in the beautiful forests of centuries-old redwoods where she spread Paula's ashes, a place she considers her sanctuary. After having fought the battle of unwanted pounds with formidable diets and calisthenics in torture chambers, she has discovered that by walking she can maintain her ideal weight and, in the process, clear her mind and practice meditation. The taste of chocolate, however, can still cause a major guilt trip—she can't resist it. The surrounding landscape, all sea and forest, invites walkers to overcome their usual resistance to disciplines beneficial to the body but wearisome when an obligation. Tabra, Isabel's artist friend whose jewelry embellishes the necks and ears of thousands of women, and who is also a character in *The Infinite Plan*, is her companion on her morning walks. Tabra has created jewelry in silver and semiprecious stones to go with the dresses Isabel wears in public appearances.

When Isabel arrived in California in 1987, she was already famous in certain circles, if unknown to the man in the street. North American universities were focusing on her novels, and critics were adjusting their literary compasses and astrolabes to position her on the map of world literature. Isabel was passing through, but William Gordon stepped out into her path, whispered the secret words that were Belisa Crepusculario's stock in trade, and the writer moved in to live with him. Isabel wins people over both in that closed space between reader and author and in the open space of the stage, where she mesmerizes her public with doses of audacity, unthreatening candor, a great deal of wit, and a powerful inner strength that issues from all the pores of this willful woman who has such an enormous aptitude for happiness.

At first she was compared to Gabriel García Márquez, and she felt flattered. She says that if she were a ballerina and someone had said she danced like Nureyev, she would have exploded with joy. But when critics persisted in that comparison, she appreciated it less. "Have you noticed that anytime a woman is successful they look for a male mentor?" She is unfazed by the opinions of reviewers, and would much rather pass an afternoon with students in her home than attend a conference of critics and authors, a situation she avoids as if it were a fate worse than death.

I can't remember when Isabel first visited my class at the end of the semester. We were at that time discussing *La casa de los espíritus*. The students, at first in a trance, couldn't break the ice and sat absolutely mute. But ice doesn't last long with Isabel. She hugged each of them, gave each an inscribed copy of her book, took pictures with all of them for their mothers, sweethearts, and grandmothers. She has visited my classes since 1988, either in my house, her house, or at the university.

"Isabel wore you out just watching her," say her friends Malú Sierra and Pía Leiva, her Chilean "sister," referring to the sixties and seventies. And she hasn't changed at all. Her success is not the work of the spirits, as she likes to say, but of a fierce Basque determination not to be defeated. She will write a page ten or fifteen times, until she is satisfied. She is a punctual and demanding worker. What she demands of herself she expects of others. She is implacable in questions of punctuality. She never makes anyone wait; she appears five minutes before the scheduled time for the meeting. She doesn't like anyone to wait on her. She prefers to take care of herself and give her attention to those who need it most.

How does this human dynamo relax? With work that occupies her hands: knitting, cooking, making note cards, making variations of the famous appliqués of the Chilean *arpilleras* (seamstresses from the period of the dictatorship), painting, making jewelry for her friends, and puppets and dolls for her grandchildren. Those grandchildren take up most of her free time. If the need is urgent, she is capable of dropping everything to take care of them. Weekends are for Willie. Her happiest hour is at night when, "in bed, in Willie's arms, we tell each other everything that has happened during the day." Isabel's office in Sausalito, twenty minutes from her house, absorbs a good part of her time. Contracts, interviews, invitations to lecture, community projects, donations, letters, phone calls, and messages flood in every day. Two assistants, answering several telephones and fax machines, never rest. She makes an engagement months, sometimes years, in advance, and unless there's an earthquake in San Francisco, or one of the grandchildren breaks out with measles while Nicolás is away, she keeps it. She never turns back once she gives her word. "Isabel's word means something," Carmen Balcells has said. Isabel enjoys iron health; she eats everything and sleeps eight uninterrupted hours from the moment her head hits the pillow.

Her nights are not for rest alone, however, because she keeps track of her dreams, and jots them down as soon as she wakes. "I get a lot of information from dreams that is useful in solving problems in my writing, learning more about myself, and managing my reality better."

For example, when she's writing she tends to have a recurrent dream about a baby. That child is always the book in process. What happens to the child in the dream usually is happening to the book in real life. "Let's say that the child is crying with a man's voice; that means I need to revise the narrative voice or tone. Other times the baby is in a room behind a closed door, and I hear him but can't reach him, or if I do, I can't get him out of the room. That means I have problems with the plot, that the story line is tangled."

Dreams also help her identify practical or emotional problems. When she dreams of a very large and messy house that she needs to clean, she wakes up knowing there is an area of her reality that needs immediate attention. "In the dream, pipes leak, beds are left unmade, dirty pots and pans clutter the kitchen, and there are piles of garbage, newspapers, dust. It's a very disturbing but very useful dream because it alerts me to aspects of my life I need to resolve."

She likes classical music, but prefers silence. It is not her habit to turn on the radio or television or play a record; she likes for others to do that. She loves movies. Willie and she watch videos of old North American and foreign films. Violent and pornographic movies aren't among them. "I've walked out of movies lots of times because I can't take the cruelty. Later, Willie tells me how it ends, with an expurgated version in which blood isn't pouring in rivers." She often goes with her husband to New York in order not to miss the theater season they love.

From her grandfather, Tata, Isabel has inherited a strength uncommon in a woman. Seeing such a small woman, one is tricked into thinking she is fragile. Just the opposite. She makes up in iron determination what she may be missing in muscle. "I was born in August, under the sign of Leo, and if I was not switched in the clinic, I have three-quarters Spanish-Basque blood, one-quarter French, and a lot of Araucan or Mapuche Indian, like everyone else in my land."

I saw that combination of Basque and Araucan blood in action when she wrested a case of champagne bottles from the trunk of her car without anyone's help and carried it upstairs into the house. On a different occasion, Isabel, her former daughter-in-law, and I, flew in a small plane to central California. Isabel was carrying Celia's guitar and a suit bag containing the dress she had worn the night before to give a lecture at Fresno State. When we got out of the plane, we had to hop onto a bus that would take us to the main terminal in San Francisco, and then climb a long flight of stairs, the risers of which were higher than normal. On the same flight was a Mexican peasant couple with three small children: two who seemed to be twins, and a little girl only slightly older than her brothers. The family seemed confused when they saw the bus, and asked us in Spanish what they should do. We told them to follow us. We made the transfer from one end of the airport to the other, and as we got off the bus, the parents each picked up one of the smaller children, leaving the little girl on her own. Without any fuss, Isabel shifted the guitar and suit bag to her left arm and scooped up the little girl with her right arm and started climbing the stairs with a firm, sure step. Someone once said that she walks as if she were carrying a water pitcher on her head. At the top of the stairs she returned the little girl to her parents and marched right ahead. I went over to them and asked, "Do you know who that lady is?" The father shook his head no. "She's a famous writer."

He didn't seem impressed. I should have told him she was a Mexican movie star. What I do know is that most of humanity goes to bed hungry and knows very little about writers. For the family that coalesced into a tribe through Isabel's art and effort, there were a number of downturns that year. Celia, the mother of Isabel's three grandchildren, was divorced from Nicolás; Jason, Willie's adopted son, left to work on the East Coast; and Ernesto, Isabel's son-in-law, was living in New Jersey. He got married the next year. Harleigh, that difficult stepchild whom Isabel loves like another son, has become a reasonable and attentive young man capable of disarming a person with his father's captivating smile. With great dedication on Isabel and Willie's part, and after a long pilgrimage through specialized schools, he has come out a winner. One day Isabel had the emotional surprise of seeing Harleigh stand in front of his whole school to say that she had taught him what love and boundaries are.

He was the same boy who, when Isabel arrived in 1987 and he was barely ten, had insisted on sleeping between Willie and her because he was afraid of the dark. Isabel coped with the matter in her way; she installed him in a sleeping bag on the floor next to the bed, with a cord tied from Harleigh's wrist to her own. Every time he felt afraid, she tugged on the cord, reminding him that she was at his side, and in that way calmed his fears. Today she uses a similar method with her grandchildren when they come to sleep at her house.

Among the many Isabels in Isabel Allende there is a little girl. Children are enchanted by her irreverence, the overflowing fantasy of her stories, the dramatic persona that possesses her when she is in front of an audience, small or large, and her facility for improvising a carnival at the least excuse. "Isabel carries her own circus with her," says Pía Leiva. "She's the delight of all children." Sometimes, to amuse herself with her listeners' scandalized reactions, she proclaims that she detests children. The truth is the complete opposite.

Lygia, the Nicaraguan housekeeper who helped Isabel take care of Paula, now helps her look after her grandchildren: Alejandro, Andrea, and Nicole. The two women have a solid friendship based on their shared chores and painful memories. Lygia tells that sometimes she thinks she has seen Paula's silhouette coming down the stairs. In fact, Paula is present everywhere in that house—in photographs, in family conversation, in everyone's memory. It is not rare to feel that her spirit is nearby.

Isabel says that Paula is a gentle presence that is with her always, like a second skin.

Writing

I have the impression you have lived from crisis to crisis. What would you do if you were condemned to a normal life?

I would have more time to meditate, and I'd get a little dog, a female.

Why female?

Because males hump table legs.

Do you think that crises created the writer you are today?

My crises, which began in my early childhood, have caused me to create a fantasy world in which I find refuge. Other people who do that end up in a mental hospital, but I've been lucky enough to have converted this private world into a product that people want to buy, something that has brought me respect instead of shock treatments. I live in reality a large part of the time, but when things turn the drab color of an ant, I can creep into my own universe, where I am sorceress and queen, and where I make the rules and change them according to my whim.

You seem to have a magic wand. Can you always escape into fiction?

Almost always. There are times, of course, like the period of Paula's tragedy, when there is no escape; then you have to sink into darkness and suffer, totally and without relief. But even in those circumstances I had the crutch of writing. In that patient, everyday exercise, I could impose order on confusion and set limits to the pain. Once you name them, events take on precise outlines and become easier to face. For example, when you say *my daughter is dying*, you define the problem. That allows you to say *I have other children, grandchildren, a husband, and a mother who love me.* Spaces take on boundaries and your anguish doesn't poison all of life.

If you could choose, would you prefer a banal life with no setbacks?

No. I realize that suffering is a condition of life; we have come into this world to lose everything, including awareness and life itself. That's how we grow up, that's how the soul matures, and that's also how we learn happiness. When you asked me whether the drama of reality feeds my books, I answer yes, it's true, but books are also the sacred place where everyday drama is raised to the category of epic and more than a personal matter becomes something I share with all humanity. In the universe of fiction, the norms are clear; suffering, violence, and terror exist, but love and solidarity prevail. That is my literary space, the world I have created in my books.

Those are fictional rules.

I've given that order to my literary world because love and solidarity are fundamental for me. I also apply those rules to my life—not always successfully, I admit. The line between the magical world of fiction and real life is very thin. As, sentence by sentence, book by book, I create that personal space in literature, I am naming and defining myself; I take the word, I exist, I become a visible being. The word makes me strong.

When King Benedict arrives at the beginning of *The Infinite Plan*, little Judy tells him they are making necklaces with magical stones. He asks what they're for. And she replies, "If you

begin to turn invisible, you put on one of these necklaces and then everyone can see you." That really struck me when I read it. In legends, heroes wear a token or drink a potion and become invisible, that is, the *opposite* of your magic. Your focus is original; the hero is invisible and has to do something to become visible. The magic philter in this case is the word, which gives him the power to exist, to be visible, to have a voice. With your words, you give life to the characters of your work, which to me seems very autobiographical.

I've had to borrow a lot from my own life for these creatures. They're voracious; they devour everything.

You worked as a journalist and on television. How did that influence your novels?

Journalism gave me nearly all the tricks I use for literature. The journalist's first duty is to snare the reader. The journalist competes with other media, with other articles in the same newspaper. He has to grab the reader's attention in the first six lines and hold him to the end. Rhythm, suspense, pace, tone, information. . . . In addition to that, he has limited space and little time, racing against the clock. It's formidable training; that immediacy and pace are useful to me in literature. Authors who haven't had that experience tend to forget that writing isn't an end in itself, it's merely a means of communication. If no one reads you, what does your work mean? I love to write, I enjoy the process, but I don't forget that there is a respondent. As a reader, if a book doesn't interest me in the first pages, I soon put it down. If I'm bored, I get irritable.

A lot of Latin American writers have been journalists: Gabriel García Márquez, Mario Vargas Llosa, Tomás Eloy Martínez.

Journalism taught me very useful techniques, such as learning to conduct an interview. When I write my novels, I normally seek models for the characters; once I find them, I tell them my intentions and proceed to tape interviews. Usually people are very generous: everyone likes to tell the story of her life. And I learned a long time ago to ask indiscreet questions; I'm shameless when it comes to prying into someone's personal life. With the good journalist's desire for objectivity, you look for both faces of the coin; you don't stop with the first version—you probe the shadows until you nose out what wasn't apparent at first. In the novel there's room to do that; you can tell a single event from many points of view. In journalism, what you want from language is effectiveness. We writers fall in love with the beauty of a sentence and lose track of the effect it produces. I am implacable about that. I cut and cut, mercilessly. Is it necessary? Or do I just like saying it? Another basic rule is not to underestimate the reader, to give him the information without hammering him over the head. Journalism makes you humble; what you write so carefully for a newspaper is used by the butcher the next day to wrap your roast. That humility can't be overlooked. Literature is like baking bread, the written word is my flour. And nothing more. Everything passes, nothing is transcendent.

And television?

If journalism is immediate, television is even more so. That image goes by without leaving a trace; you can't even wrap meat in it. I suppose that on television I learned to be brief and to think in images, something that can be very useful in novels. I like for the reader to see, to experience scenes as if he were watching a screen. I think in TV terms: first, I introduce the characters, create the atmosphere and tension, then develop the action, and that leads to the end.

Did someone teach you that?

You learn as you go. When does a play or television drama work? When the characters are coherent, simple without being simpleminded, when the plot is accessible and develops rhythmically, when there is tension, suspense, and a memorable denouement. If everything happens on one plane, it doesn't work, and it doesn't work in a novel, either.

You also wrote plays. What did you learn from that?

Actors taught me to be consistent in creating characters. Each actor studies his role in depth in order to make it credible. Let's say he has to appear on the stage for a few seconds to announce that dinner is served. He asks himself, who am I? Why am I working as a waiter? Do I like this job? What is my past? In that way he can develop his character and say that dinner is served in a convincing way. My first play, written in 1970, was called *The Ambassador*. It was the story of three guerrillas who kidnap an ambassador and keep him prisoner in a cellar where they all have to live in close quarters. They talk, share, remember, plan, fight, reconcile, suffer the same tensions, are equally bored, learn to listen to one another, respect one another, and end up as friends. Then they have to kill him. Those were times when guerrilla warfare was being waged all across the continent. Socialism had just triumphed in Chile, the first time that a Marxist, Salvador Allende, had come to power through a democratic vote. We thought the world was going to change. We had just lived through the dreams of '68, with the student uprisings in Paris and Germany; there was an upsurge of revolutionary ideas, and it was also the spring of the hippies. People were in the streets, there were murals of doves and flowers, we were singing protest songs. I was twenty-eight years old and felt I owned the world. My humor column and TV program allowed me into Chileans' homes every week; people greeted me in the street; I felt loved and accepted; I was full of the strength and sauciness given to the young. I had so much to say on the class struggle, socialist ideals, the justification of violence in systems that exploited the masses, that my head was spinning. I sprinkled all that into the guerrillas' monologues in the play; the poor actors had to say all the things I was dying to tell. One of them, Alejandro Cohen, played the part of a young worker who had gotten into the guerrilla war out of desperation, unlike the intellectuals of the group, students who were there for idealistic reasons. When Alejandro read his part aloud for the first time, he told me that workers didn't talk like that, that he felt ridiculous saying such things; his motivation was survival, poverty, action, not oratory. I had to rewrite his part completely. Now when I develop a character, I always remember Alejandro and ask myself: Is that how this character talks? Is his behavior appropriate for his character? For his life?

Where did you get the idea for that work?

That was the first time I'd ever had what they call "a stroke of inspiration." The muse appeared—swathed in veils and flitting about like an obese dragonfly—and put the gift in my hands. President Allende had named my stepfather ambassador to Argentina. Someone joked to him, "Don't get kidnapped, Ramón," because in Uruguay, the Tupamaros had recently kidnapped a diplomat. That comment hit me like a ton of bricks. I had a violent physical reaction; I vomited, I became dehydrated, and I broke out in hives. Too bad that never happened again, because I lost several kilos in three days. I sat down at the typewriter and wrote the play in that length of time. I didn't rest or eat until I typed *The End*. Then I gave it to Malú Gatica, a very popular actress in Chile, who saw it had possibilities, and with great generosity—seeing there was no part for her—she showed it to La Compañía de los Cuatro. Two weeks later we had the project on track. I went to rehearsals every night, and at dawn the following morning would incorporate the corrections and suggestions of the director and the actors. In a few weeks' time I learned what takes years in formal classes.

Is there a great difference between spoken and written dialogue? In your stories your dialogues are very brief. What place does dialogue have in your work?

Minimal. For dialogue to be credible it has to be colloquial; it has to be the way the people in that place and that time really speak. Language is a living animal, organic, that changes and dies. People in Chile no longer speak the way they did in the seventies. If in *The House of the Spirits* I had used the slang of that period, it would be incomprehensible today. That also makes translations more difficult and excludes readers who are unfamiliar with those idioms. Colloquial dialogue, especially among young people, changes constantly. I try to set my stories in a nonspecific, often mythic, time and place, where they will stay fresh. Colloquial dialogue anchors the story in reality.

So the fact that your work is free of local slang may be one of the reasons why your translations work?

Absolutely. What North Americans call *slang* and we call *jerga* or *argot* is untranslatable. In *The Infinite Plan,* I had a lot of problems in that regard, because in the Latino barrio where Gregory Reeves grows up, they didn't speak a true Spanish but, rather, a hybrid form called *pachuco.* And then in the chapter on Vietnam, I found that during the war a whole language evolved; terms were used that everyone in the United States recognized but no one else in the world. Should I write those phrases in English? The words didn't translate to Spanish—the only language I can write fiction in. If I didn't use slang, the narrative would lose credibility. So I avoided dialogue, and when I used local expressions, I did it in a context in which the meaning could be deduced.

Do you believe in the exclusive power of inspiration?

Inspiration is a wonderful thing that sometimes happens almost as a miracle, like falling in love at first sight, or winning the lottery. Inspiration produces an extraordinary energy that occasionally allows you to reach the clouds. But literature is more hard work than anything else. When I've had to teach at some university, I tell my students that writing is like athletic training: you have to do it every day, with perseverance and humility. The athlete knows the hours that go into training that no one sees or appreciates will help him reach his competitive goals; without that discipline he can't win. Every draft the author writes, every page that ends up in the wastebasket, is indispensable in producing a publishable paragraph.

James Baldwin said he couldn't write anywhere but Paris, while Faulkner claimed that he couldn't write anywhere but home. Have your surroundings affected your creation?

Maybe not in the short term, but in the long run, yes. I wrote my first two novels, which have the taste and smell of Chile, in Venezuela. They are nostalgic books. I needed many years in the Caribbean to absorb its color and write *Eva Luna*. The stories, which like the novel are Caribbean, I wrote in the United States. I was living here, but I still had the countryside of Venezuela deep inside me. *The Infinite Plan* took four years to write; I couldn't do it in less because I had to have time to feel California on my skin. A place determines a state of mind, but not necessarily a narrative. I can still write about Chile; I can select themes that took place in the past. But I can't write about places I don't know, as Jules Verne did. Nor can I go to India for a few weeks and return with a novel about the Taj Mahal.

Distance and nostalgia seem to fire your creativity. That was how you wrote *The House of the Spirits*. Could you have written that exact book in Chile, calmly, living a comfortable life?

No, that novel is an attempt to recreate a world I'd lost. Which is also true of *Of Love and Shadows*. I carry a Chile inside me that is frozen in time, in the seventies, and now when I go there, many years later, I don't recognize it. Sometimes I find it in a fishing village, or in a miner's house in the north, but everything has changed. For me, the landscape of Chile is the one Pablo Neruda describes. When I go to Isla Negra, I don't see the Pacific Ocean. I see the infinite sea of the poet's verses. Not the real landscape but the landscape of the word.

Do you have a more exact vision of events when viewed from a distance or from close up?

From a distance. Sometimes the distance is geographical and other times it's temporal. I've never been able to write in the eye of the hurricane, except in the case of *Paula*, which I wrote as events were happening, sitting in a corridor of a hospital in Madrid and later beside her bed in my home in California.

You move comfortably in and out of several genres: journalism, novel, short story, essay, memoir. Have you tried poetry?

Never. For that you need genius.

Fiction is your forte. How did you feel writing a memoir?

I suppose that memoirs are written as an exercise in nostalgia, but in my case it was an act of survival. A memoir is always subjective; that links it to fiction, because the act of selecting what to tell and what to omit is a kind of fiction. You choose what to highlight and what to hide, as well as the light in which things are presented. With those advantages, anyone can turn into a protagonist with a special destiny. You tell the brightest and darkest moments because no one wastes pages writing about the infinite shades of gray in which most of life occurs. The difficulty in *Paula* wasn't in selecting events, since I had no interest in looking better than I am—that book was born as a letter for my daughter, who knew me very, very, well—but in trying to be honest without betraying the persons who appear in the book under their true names. That dilemma between loyalty to writing and loyalty to the persons I am fond of still torments me.

García Márquez said that the day he had to kill Colonel Aureliano Buendía he cried for two hours. Do you get dangerously close to your characters? Have you suffered a painful separation from any of them?

I have. When Clara del Valle died in *The House of the Spirits*, I didn't know what to do; without her, the story lost its soul. She was my favorite character. I didn't have to invent her—she was my grandmother. Fortunately, her spirit came back to wander through the second part of the novel, because if she hadn't, I would still be trying to end the thing. There are other characters I can never let go because they come back in disguise—for example, Riad Halabí, the Turk in *Eva Luna*. In my stories there are often similar characters, other names and other faces, some man defeated by his own good heart. Where did Riad Halabí come from? I don't know anyone like that; he simply appeared in the pages of *Eva Luna*, alive, real, with his harelip, his Levantine eyes, and his coffee-colored suit, and possessed me.

You didn't know anyone like that in Lebanon?

No.

And your female protagonists—do they have traits in common?

Yes, many of them do, but not the men. Esteban Trueba isn't at all like Francisco Leal, nor is he like Riad Halabí or Gregory Reeves.

But Francisco Leal reminds me a little of Rolf Carlé. Although they are different in the way they love. In *Of Love and Shadows,* Irene is everything to Francisco; he loves her with a total and exclusive love; passionate and tender, he is the ideal romantic. Rolf Carlé, on the other hand, has those rosy-cheeked cousins who waft through his dreams trailing the scent of cinnamon and lemon. His love for Eva Luna is not like Francisco's for Irene. Francisco Leal is Latin, and Rolf Carlé is European; do you think the difference in commitment is due to cultural traits?

No, it's more that Francisco and Irene love each other in tragic circumstances. Death is always hovering over them, lurking about. The quality of their love is determined by the danger in which they live. There's no time for frivolities, only the transcendental, and that's why they love with such urgency and total dedication—like the protagonists, for example, of Hemingway's *For Whom the Bell Tolls.*

A book completed is a slayed lion. Do you lose interest once a book is published?

I forget the characters, the theme. Years later people come and ask me details about them, and I don't know what they're talking about. I can remember, barely, the titles of the novels, but I haven't a clue about the short stories.

What conditions do you like when you write? Talk to me about method and craft.

I've been able to write in any situation, whatever I need to do. It's like the first flames of love: if there's no other way, you do it behind doors. A large part of *Paula* was written by hand in the hospital or the hotel. *The Stories of Eva Luna* I wrote on lined paper, unobtrusively, in my room or Willie's office, because I didn't have a room of my own, to use Virginia Woolf's words. *The House of the Spirits* was written night after night on the kitchen table. The ideal is to write in my study, surrounded by photographs of people I love and the beneficent spirits that are always with me, with a burning candle to summon light and fresh flowers from my garden, in complete solitude and silence. But I could work without all that. Most important is silence. *Daughter of Fortune* and *Portrait in Sepia* were written in my house in San Rafael.

Do you like background music? That's in style now. People need it in restaurants, stores, elevators.

Usually, it bothers me. To me, noise is the worst form of pollution. Silence is fruitful, and generous . . . a luxury more and more difficult to find.

Marta Traba tirelessly cleaned closets to put off the moment of starting to write. García Márquez puts on overalls and repairs the electrical outlets of his house, or paints the doors green. What do you do before January 8, the day you know you have to start another book?

I clean and straighten the space where I am going to write. I remove everything connected with the previous book and place around me the things I need for the new project. Disorder really bothers me. I check drawers, files, closets, bookshelves, and when I have everything the way I want it and there are no more excuses and I have no choice but to begin, I sit down to write. That's why I have an official date for starting a book: January 8. That way I can't put it off forever. Beginning a book is always frightening, because it's a journey without a map.

Are you productive? How much do you write in a day, for example?

Less and less. I've become very critical of my work. I go through a lot of drafts; I correct until I'm so tired that the page wins. I never lack for ideas; stories pour out like raging torrents, but telling them cleanly is a daunting task.

Is it like an inexhaustible reservoir you have dammed up and on January 8 you open the floodgate and let it all out?

The only time I have felt empty was after writing *Paula*. My reserves had been exhausted. I was dried up inside and felt that life had no meaning. I wanted to die. I was frightened by that sterile silence, that absence of inner voices, of images, of stories. I had always believed that the ether is filled with stories and that my job was to tune my ear to hear them, but I had become deaf.

It seems that all writers experience blocks; it's inevitable. How did you get out of yours?

When I realized that I was blocked on fiction, I started writing *Aphrodite*. I could move around in that subject comfortably—it was a matter of researching, reading, even cooking. My mother came to live with me for two months, and we devoted ourselves to testing the recipes that appear in the book. My house smelled like paradise. . . .

A dream pulled me from that paralysis I felt in regard to fiction. I jot down dreams that seem meaningful, because they help me understand my reality and reach decisions. *Paula* brought an avalanche of letters from readers; the mail kept me occupied for nearly two years. One day I dreamed about four Indians emerging from the heart of the South American continent bearing a litter holding a large coffer as a gift for a conquistador. That man seemed impatient. His gloved hand—which was at the same time my hand—was writing in longhand: *If you open the box, you will suffer an invisible wound from which your life will flow out in strings of words.* In the meantime, the Indians were crossing sierras, mountains, jungles, rivers, and everywhere they went the world fell silent. I saw brightly colored birds moving their beaks but heard no song; I saw rushing streams but did not hear them roar: jungle, people, towns—everything was muted. The conquistador's gift was devouring the sounds of the world, swallowing up the words. What was in that mysterious box? A beautiful young girl? Gold, diamonds? A pitcher of sacred water from the fountain of youth? I didn't know the meaning of the dream and didn't want to tarnish it with psychoanalytic theories, but I decided that I should travel to the heart of the continent in search of the coffer.

And that's why you went to the Amazon River?

Yes. It took me a year to plan the trip, but finally, in 1996, I was able to go. I don't need to tell you about that adventure now. It's enough to say that I swam naked in the Negro River infested with piranhas, ate roast crocodile and boiled porcupine, slept with a spider monkey, and saw a man killed before my eyes. He was shot five times in the head. I didn't find the four Indians with the voracious coffer that held all sounds and stories, but when I got back home, I brought with me that vast planet of water, green and warm, like a treasure. On January 8, 1997, the long silence of mourning ended, and I could begin to write fiction again. That day I turned on my computer and wrote the first sentence of a story that had nothing to do with Indians, the Amazon, or a conquistador.

Why do you think that the dream determined your writing?

Maybe the interpretation would be that I was inside that coffer, traveling through hostile and dangerous territory, like the territory of death where I had been with Paula. I was locked in a dark box, in silence; I was transported by bearers and had no control over anything. But I wasn't totally passive: I was absorbing the sounds of the world, words and stories, replenishing my reserves. Maybe the conquistador represented the moment when I could reconquer my space through the written word. Don't you think that might be the message of the gloved hand writing a warning that my life would flow out in strings of words? I don't know, Celia. Whatever the explanation, the dream motivated me to travel, and the journey inspired me to write.

Who are the people who have helped you in the artistic aspect of literature, helped you become a writer?

No one. I never took literature classes, I've never participated in literary workshops, I have never worked with an editor who listened to my doubts or guided me. I don't belong to clubs or literary groups; usually, those are male purviews—we women writers are very isolated. No one critiques my work before it's published except my mother, whose comments are more human than literary. Nor has anyone ever given me a subject. People tell me their life stories, or write me to suggest a topic, but I can't use them because I have to feel it in me; it has to resonate like an echo of my memory, my experiences, my emotions.

Literary creation "incarnates," becomes flesh, and then comes the painful process of giving birth.

That process isn't painful, it's always joyful, even if the subject is difficult and the writing slow, at times depleting. Each book is a very personal journey. Why do I choose those characters and not others? Why such urgency to tell the story and not another? Because deep down, I am exploring a shadowy space of the past, of memory, of my character, of my soul. In the laborious daily exercise of writing, I shed light into those dark corners and, with a little luck, come to understand my own reality a little better.

And finally, Isabel, why do you write?

I suppose that writing is an attempt to understand life's confusion, to make the world more bearable, and, if possible, to change it. Why do I write? Because I am filled with stories that demand to be told, because the words are choking me, because I like and need to write, because if I don't write, my soul dries up and I die.

Daughter of Fortune

Hija de la fortuna was published in Barcelona in November 1998 by Plaza y Janés. Italian and German editions quickly followed in 1999. HarperCollins in London distributed the English-language version in the United Kingdom, including Australia and New Zealand.

Daughter of Fortune was published by HarperCollins in the United States in October 1999, translated into English by Margaret Sayers Peden, the translator of all Isabel's previous books with the exception of *The House of the Spirits.* Spanish, Italian, German, Portuguese, and Dutch editions drew major attention in Europe and Spanish America. Sales numbered in the hundreds of thousands within a few months of publication. Immediate reprints placed it on many best-seller lists: in Spain, ABC ranked it number one.

The celebration in 1999 of the 150th anniversary of the discovery of gold and the avalanche of adventurers that discovery brought with it provided an excuse for some critics to claim the work and its author as part of California's patrimony. A passage describing a battle between a bear and a bull—a brutal entertainment the miners enthusiastically adopted for lack of a bullring like those in Mexico—reflects the ambiance of those early adventurers who arrived in droves in search of gold. The author's energy in depicting the ferocious encounter between the two very different animals augments the suspense of the tale, evoking the strengths and weaknesses of each beast as it attacks and parries the other before the eyes of the crowd inflamed by the sight of blood. "At the third blast of the trumpet, a wood gate was raised and a young, gleaming, black bull trotted into the ring, snorting. For an instant the gallery was silenced with an awe and then a full-throated 'Ole!' engulfed the animal . . . the bull trotted completely around the ring, confused, while the crowd egged him on with catcalls; he charged again, trying to lift the bear with his horns, but the bear took its punishment without moving, until he saw his chance and with one sure slash tore open the bull's nose. The wounded, disoriented bull attacked the bear again and again, charging, making blind thrusts, but finally lost the battle. Suddenly the bear rose up and grasped the bull's neck in a terrible embrace, clamping his teeth in its flesh. For long moments they danced together around the circle described by the chain [about the bear's neck] while the sand grew red with blood and the galleries echoed with the yells of men."

Because of the bizarre nature of the encounter and the swift pace of the action, this passage leaves the reader dazed with blood and the horror of death.

For many, however, this novel will be a love story. For others it will be the search for identity of a woman in love, but oppressed by the social order from which she escapes in order to weave her own destiny. Tao Chi'en, who turns gradually into the main character, similarly breaches the barrier of his traditional inferiority.

In all her work, Isabel Allende has insisted on a certain ideal of freedom: freedom from the confines of the patriarchal system during her days as a journalist in Chile; political freedom and the necessary denunciation of the military dictatorship in Chile; and individual freedom to pursue a personal identity. Isabel's own life, like that of Eliza Sommers, a long pilgrimage, has always been a quest for freedom.

Each reader will, with the author, create the novel according to his or her own interpretation—hence, the diversity of critical judgments. The chimera of gold, the mirage that attracted so many adventurers, led the author to consider two possible titles, *Wheel of Fortune* and *Fool's Gold*, which ultimately were discarded in favor of *Daughter of Fortune*. The journey begun in 1982 is apparently completed in the year 2000. *Portrait in Sepia* was published in Spain, Chile, and Argentina in October and November 2000. This is the second part of a trilogy started by *Daughter of Fortune* and finished by *The House of the Spirits*.

What was the spark that ignited your imagination in regard to a historical novel about the days of the Gold Rush?

I really can't say. I suppose that when I came to live in California, following my love, I was struck by the first spark. After all, *Daughter of Fortune* is the story of a Chilean woman who travels across half the world and ends up in California, all for love. In that, Eliza is like me. But that's a romantic explanation that may have nothing to do with reality. I think that by the time I finished writing *The Infinite Plan,* in 1991, I was already enthusiastic about California. In order to write that book, I'd had to do research on this area, its geography and history. I read about the Gold Rush of 1848 and imagined how life must have been in those days. I learned that many Chileans came to California with the hope of getting rich in the placers, and so little by little the idea for the novel began to take shape. I planned to begin writing on January 8, 1992, but on that date my daughter Paula was in a coma in a Madrid hospital. That was to be the worst year of my life, a year of pure pain and shattered hopes. On January 8, 1993, still submersed in mourning the death of my daughter, I began *Paula*. Then came a long period of drought; following that, I wrote *Aphrodite*, because the idea of returning to fiction terrified me. I suppose that *Aphrodite* pulled me from the swamp I was bogged down in and restored my energy, because on January 8, 1998, I launched right into the novel.

I see the process of the historical research as taking place on several planes: California, Chile, Chinese culture both in the homeland and in California. Did you follow some specific methodology? Did you encounter reefs or obstacles in particular that are worthy of mention?

During the seven years between *The Infinite Plan* and *Daughter of Fortune,* I immersed myself fully in California history. I read everything I could get my hands on, and watched documentaries, videos, and television programs. I can't say I did so with any method, because I didn't know what I was looking for. I don't have an outline or preconceived idea when I write, but feel my way along, like a blind man walking on unfamiliar terrain. Facts that seemed important to me, colorful characters, curious events, I put down in notebooks and on those yellow Post-Its, which I stuck all around the walls of my office. When finally I sat down to write, the room was filled with little bits of stuck-on notes and books with marked pages. I had become so familiar with the details that it was as if I had lived in the place in that era. I came to believe that I was the reincarnation of someone who had known Eliza Sommers and Tao Chi'en in 1850, and that my only task was to report what I knew. Later, as the novel was developing—almost as if under a spell—I had to check aspects of the research that were missing, but that was easy because everything I needed was available in the magnificent libraries here in California. As I incorporated information, I took down the yellow notes from the walls and put away the books stacked on the floor. When there were no Post-Its or bookmarks left, the novel was complete.

Tao Chi'en turned out to be one of the male protagonists in your work who is characterized by his tenderness toward the women they love: Francisco Leal, Rolf Carlé, even Gregory Reeves, despite his early false starts. Where did you get the idea for the character Tao Chi'en, and how does he differ from the other characters I mentioned?

Tao Chi'en is one of those surprising characters who sneak in the backdoor and take over the whole stage. I have to have a reason for having a young girl like Eliza Sommers abandon the security of her family to follow an evasive lover. In those days, her love affair, and certainly her pregnancy, was tantamount to dishonor, to social death. Eliza leaves because she has nothing to lose—she has already lost everything in the eyes of her family and the society in which she lives. To stow away on a ship, she would have to have an accomplice. Any sailor would do, and the idea of using someone Chinese came almost by chance. But Eliza couldn't show up in California with a baby; she had to have a miscarriage on shipboard. I realized then that to be able to help, her accessory would have to know something about medicine, and so I had to transform the sailor into a physician. That part of the research took months, because I had to learn about Eastern medicine—and that made the Tao Chi'en character much more complex. Once he took shape, he grew and grew and I couldn't get rid of him. Page by page, Tao Chi'en was taking over the novel, and I think that in the end he is more the protagonist than Eliza herself. He is very much like some of the male characters in my earlier novels: Jaime in *The House of the Spirits*, the Leal brothers in *Of Love and Shadows*, Riad Halabí in *Eva Luna*, and *The Stories of Eva Luna*. They are strong, compassionate, generous men who come to the rescue of the female protagonists, who gamble everything to help others—men defeated by their good hearts. They're father substitutes taking the place of the father missing from all my books. Each of them has something of Tío Ramón, the adoptive father who fell into my life like a gift from heaven.

Some readers have called the *Daughter of Fortune* a novel of magical realism. Aside from Lin's appearance to Tao Chi'en, and the business of carrying ice from Valparaíso to San Francisco on board one of the first steamships, what other magical realism do you see in the novel?

I don't think there is *any* magical realism. The apparition of Lin's spirit can be explained by the character of Tao Chi'en, who firmly believes in the existence of spirits and who deeply loves the woman death had torn from him. He calls her so strongly in his thoughts that she appears to him, the way my daughter Paula appears at every bend of the road. The story about the ice is totally realistic. There was, in fact, a Chilean who in 1849 carried ice from Chile to San Francisco aboard a sailing ship. To make it more credible, I wrote that he brought it on a steamship. Not a shred of magical realism. Things that in the novel seem to be the product of a pathological imagination are, in fact, historical events, such as the slave girls in Chinatown, the cut-off ears, the whites' abuses against other races, the women who passed as men, and much more.

In the second part of the novel there are suspenseful passages centering on the wretched Eliza, buried in the belly of the ship, bleeding to death from her miscarriage, with no one to help her but Tao Chi'en, who literally drags her from death at the last moment. Could that have happened in that time?

The enormous leap made by medicine is very recent, coming only after the advent of anesthesia and antiseptics in the mid-nineteenth century. When the railroad across the United States was being built, the Chinese work crews had their own physicians because they had no faith in the white doctors and their barbaric procedures. The Chinese boiled water to prevent cholera, dysentery, and other illnesses when North American doctors still did not know to wash their hands or disinfect their instruments before operating. Tao Chi'en uses the resources within his reach to save Eliza: to provoke contractions to expel every vestige of her pregnancy, to stop the hemorrhaging, to strengthen her immune system, and to force her to eat and sleep. If Eliza had contracted an infection, that would have been that, and the Chinese physician couldn't have done anything to save her.

You write beautiful descriptions of the sea and of the battle against the shark. Where did all that come from?

In a book by Vicente Pérez Rosales, there's a passing reference to their having "caught a shark," and that sent my imagination flying. Have you seen a shark? They're formidable creatures! It takes them a long time to die after they're taken out of the water; the idea of a shark agonizing on the deck of one of those tiny, fragile ships left me sleepless for several nights. The descriptions of the sea, I suppose, are the sum of personal experiences and haphazard readings.

Do you think Tao Chi'en's generosity and self-sacrifice are plausible? What inspired you to create that character?

Of course they're plausible! I believe that people have an enormous capacity for altruism and courage, both men and women. I also believe in hopelessly evil individuals. That's typical of my characters. These are the people I find most interesting in this world: the noblest souls and the worst villains. The inspiration for Tao Chi'en comes from several friends: Dr. Benjamín Viel, who was one of the heroes of my childhood; Dr. Arturo Jirón, one of Salvador Allende's doctors, who was captured in the burning La Moneda palace during the 1973 military coup in Chile, and who then spent years in a concentration camp on Dawson Island; Dr. Miki Shima, a specialist in acupuncture and Eastern medicine, who was at Paula's side during the long months of her dying. All of those men are generous, brave, and compassionate; they are men with great hearts, dedicated to the service of others.

Getting back to Eliza, it seems to me that the true protagonist of your work isn't a woman this time. I feel Tao Chi'en is better defined, stronger, more resolute. Does that have something to do with the nineteenth century?

As I said earlier, Tao Chi'en simply took over the novel. I don't think it has anything to do with the fact that nineteenth-century women had no voice and no vote, as we say in Chile. Eliza is a defiant woman, courageous in her decisions, but don't forget that an important facet of her personality is her discretion, her ability to make herself invisible, not to be noticed. She is a silent person who observes and acts, but makes no noise. Maybe that's why she seems less defined or less strong than Tao Chi'en—but think of all she does, and of the period she does it in. She lived in the middle of the Victorian era, when women were less than shadows in a patriarchal world.

Do you think you wrote the novel you set out to write, or did it turn out different?

I don't "set out" to write anything. My novels write themselves as I go, word by word. For me it's a feat to finish them; it never occurs to me that they might have been different.

How many years did it take for the plot of *Daughter of Fortune* to incubate, and in what way did its gestation differ from others of your novels?

All my novels require a long period of gestation; that seems to be inescapable. Ideas begin to form inside me and gradually grow in my womb, not my head. It's an organic, slow, uncontrollable process. Sometimes I'm not aware that I'm carrying a creature inside me until it begins to choke me; other times I feel the delicious tickling of a novel kicking its feet to be born. *Daughter of Fortune* took seven years to take on flesh: a pregnancy from Mars.

Why did you let your irresistible sense of humor stay almost buried in this novel?

It wasn't intentional. Every story has its tone, its manner of being told. Humor can't be forced, just as you can't repeat the formula that worked in the previous novel. In this novel there are no elements of magical realism or political harangue because they weren't relevant; in the same way, I suppose, the tone had to be measured. Look, Celia, I could look for a clever way to answer that question, but let's be honest—nothing funny came to mind.

Your readers find you more subdued as a writer, less disposed to hyperbole and outlandish fantasy, and with less passion in your protagonist. Why did you tone down the distinctive characteristics of a style that has made you famous throughout the world?

Because I'm older. I've changed; I've matured; I'm not comfortable with exaggeration as I once was.

I know that this novel is selling at a frantic pace. From November 1998 to this day, *Daughter of Fortune* keeps selling in every language. It may stay back to back with *Portrait in Sepia,* just published in October 2000. How does that compare with *The House of the Spirits,* or with *Paula?*

The books help one another. *The House of the Spirits* was the first, and had an unexpected success; let's say it had a reception not often seen in the world of literature. The strange thing is that it keeps right on going: for fifteen years it has been in bookstores in several languages. That success is cumulative and has benefited the other books. It would be unfair to compare the last with the first, because the most recent has traveled a road paved by those that went before it.

Is your mother happy with the ending of this most recent novel?

No, my mother wanted a clear and definitive ending—just as you did, as I recall. But I'm sorry, it wouldn't work. When I wrote the sentence "I am free," I realized that this novel isn't a romantic story but a story about gaining freedom. The open ending seemed the only one possible.

Tell me the truth. Was Eliza's Andieta the legendary Joaquín Murieta, the Chilean or Mexican—it isn't known which—Robin Hood who devastated California during the Gold Rush? Did you consult John Rollin Ridge's novel *The Life and Adventures of Joaquín Murieta* (1854), or Pablo Neruda's play *Fulgor y Muerte de Joaquín Murieta?*

Joaquín Murieta was a legend. It's possible there were several Mexican or Chilean bandits known by the name *Joaquín*. We do know that Captain Harry Love killed a band of several Mexicans. He cut off one's head, and another's hand, and returned to San Francisco with his trophies, claiming they belonged to Joaquín Murieta and his second-in-command. Ridge, a newspaperman, wrote a popular novel about a half-invented bandit, creating a legend. The story of Murieta has been told many times. I felt free to tell it once more, from a different angle.

How do you see Eliza's odyssey compared with that of a woman of today?

We could say that Eliza's adventure is allegory of the feminist movement: the woman leaves the prison of domesticity, and the corset, and sets forth to conquer a purely masculine world; in order to do that, she learns to use the weapons and tools of men; she must masculinize herself, but once she gains her freedom she returns to her female role—*without* the corset and *with* new power. A century and a half ago, in Eliza's era, women had nothing; they were totally dependent on fathers and husbands. If they had the misfortune to have to work, the closest man in the family took charge of her salary because it was supposed that a woman "had no head for money." The woman was fated to be "silent, pregnant, and shoeless in her home," as the popular saying goes. That is, she couldn't make a decision, not even about her own body or soul. She was trained for her role as a mother—again, something she had no control over—and had no possessions. Still today, in the third millennium, women around the world are the poorest of the poor. You and I, Celia, are in the minority of privileged women. We must never forget that.

Are you happy with *Daughter of Fortune?* You more than anyone make me think of what Hemingway said: "A completed book is a slayed lion," and once dead is never spoken of again.

Exactly right. A slayed lion. I can't reread my books. Once they leave my hands, they no longer belong to me, and I prefer to forget them. So, am I happy with this novel? I don't know. I did my part in writing it. I'm happy if reading it provides several hours of entertainment for its readers. All I want to do is my best; I don't go around worrying about posterity. As an English writer said: "What has posterity done for me?"

Portrait in Sepia*

With *Portrait in Sepia*, published in the year 2000, Isabel Allende continues the saga initiated in *Daughter of Fortune*, 1998. Historically and politically these two novels would culminate in *The House of the Spirits*, 1982, the author's masterpiece, forming an ambitious narrative trilogy on the Chilean families during a period of more than a century and a half. The long journey by sea from Valparaíso to California takes place during the Gold Rush of 1849 in *Daughter of Fortune*. Instead, *Portrait in Sepia* begins in San Francisco in the first chapter, but in the next two chapters the action moves to Chile. *The House of the Spirits* takes place in Chile from the beginning of the twentieth century to the time of the military coup and the fall of Chile's first socialist president, Salvador Allende, in 1973. The book ends during the initial stages of the military government led by General Augusto Pinochet, who remained in power until 1990.

There are differences between these three historical novels. In *The House of the Spirits*, written during the military despotism, indirect references are made to Chile without ever naming the country directly. However, it can be recognized by geographical descriptions, the names of places in the capital, and allusions to political and literary figures who were of national prominence. Advances in technology, the automobile and the airplane, the two world wars, the earthquake in the city of Chillán act as signposts of the passing of time in the novel. In both *Daughter of Fortune* and *Portrait in Sepia*, the action unfolds within the framework of direct historical and geo-

*Translation of this chapter by Roland Hamilton.

graphical references. *The House of the Spirits* is shrouded by the literary technique of magic realism and by its eccentric characters; nevertheless in the end it passes judgment on the military regime of Pinochet, whom the reader can easily recognize. Pinochet is present as an ominous shadow, but he never appears in person.

Aurora del Valle, born in 1880, starts to tell her story at thirty years of age with retrospective visions of her past. She says, "Because of my dreams, I am different, like people who because of a genetic illness or some deformity have to make a constant effort to live a normal life. They bear visible signs: mine can not be seen, but it exists." From California, she moves to Chile with her grandmother Paulina.

Aurora del Valle arrives in Chile almost at the same time as the great poet Rubén Darío, who with the aid of President Balmaceda manages to publish the first edition of *Azul* in 1888 in Valparaíso, which initiated the literary movement of Spanish American Modernismo. The capital, Santiago, in 1887 was "a tranquil, sleepy city, which smelled of a mixture of flowering jasmine and horse manure" according to the inimitable narrative voice of Isabel.

The War of the Pacific during 1879–1883, the revolution against President Balmaceda in 1891, serve as historical markers in the novel. The description of Caleufú in southern Chile, the hacienda of the Domínguez family where Diego takes Aurora to live with his parents and the rest of the family, is achieved with strong brush strokes of vibrant colors, in contrast to the accelerated pace of the wars with their violence, as the author pauses to contemplate the sensual delight of the Chilean landscape.

The presidency of José Manuel Balmaceda, 1886–1891, is judged today by historians differently than in Chile at the time. During his period in office irreconcilable ruptures came to the fore between liberals and conservatives, bringing about a revolution that broke out in January of 1891 and lasted until September of the same year. More Chileans died during the conflict than in the War of the Pacific when Chile fought against Perú and Bolivia. Today, historians consider Balmaceda one of Chile's most progressive presidents. Unfortunately, he committed suicide in the Argentine Embassy at

Santiago when he found out his side had lost on September 19, 1891. He was only fifty-one years old.

Isabel Allende succeeds in creating moments of suspense immersed in the traditions of Chilean families of the nineteenth century, enclosed in their large colonial houses where the inhabitants are born, marry, receive religious sacraments, and die amidst the murmur of prayers and secretive whispering. They flee from Santiago and take refuge in their lordly country estates which are like fortresses for numerous members of the family of Paulina del Valle, while those loyal to Balmaceda search for possible members of the opposition in order to assassinate them.

The trilogy of *Daughter of Fortune, Portrait in Sepia,* and *The House of the Spirits* introduces a series of strong and resolute women who undergo vicissitudes, embark on pilgrimages to far-away places, or journeys into their psyche, to finally find their true identities and fulfill their destinies.

You have published two novels, *Daughter of Fortune* in 1999 and now *Portrait in Sepia*, during the relatively short period of two years. Tell me about the process of gestation.

Daughter of Fortune started developing during the seven years after the death of my daughter. After that tragedy I became very depressed; it was not very noticeable in everyday activities, because I continued leading a normal life, but it manifested itself in my lack of creativity. I could not write novels for a long time; it was as if my imagination had weathered completely. The idea of a novel about the Gold Rush in California had been haunting me since 1991, but every time I tried to write it I would run into a formidable wall of silence. I was empty inside; I lacked the strength and the inspiration to embark upon the project, in spite of the fact that I was doing in-depth research on the subject, and I had plenty of material. Finally, after writing *Aphrodite*, I overcame that grief which was pulling me down as if I had a millstone tied to my feet, and I was able to return to writing fiction. Perhaps during those dry years the playful energy necessary to write novels had been accumulating, because as soon as I fin-

ished *Daughter of Fortune* I was ready to start another book, and
since then I have written two more books; one of them has not been
published yet.

**If *Daughter of Fortune* was inspired by the 49ers—the anniver-
sary of the Gold Rush—what was the spark that set off *Portrait
in Sepia*?**

I wanted to tell about the second half of the nineteenth century
in Chile, a passionate time in Chilean history. It was a violent century. First Chile was at war with Spain until achieving independence;
then there were never-ending battles against the indigenous people,
to the point where they were almost exterminated. We also attacked
our neighbors, Peru and Bolivia, in the War of the Pacific, when we
took vast tracts of land from those countries. Moreover, we had a
very bloody revolution in 1891, during the presidency of Balmaceda. I suppose that every book derives from some personal preoccu-
pation, although often one does not discover the exact nature of that
concern until long after the book has been finished. I thought that the
theme of *Portrait in Sepia* would be war, which interested me as a
way of understanding the nature of Chileans, but now I realize that
the theme of the book is memory. Aurora del Valle, the main character, is a young lady with a blank page in her past; she does not
remember the first years of her life, partly because her paternal
grandmother, a Chilean matron, took it upon herself to erase those
memories. There is a very traumatic and violent episode which cuts
Aurora's life in half, and nothing is ever the same for her. Her past
disappears behind a curtain of silence. At the beginning of the book,
Aurora is a weak character, but as she searches for her identity and
tries to recover the lost memory and battles with phantoms in black
pajamas from her nightmares, she develops precise dimensions,
which lead her to become a strong and decisive woman.

The course of Aurora del Valle's development can be seen to
symbolize Chile, a country that suffered a brutal trauma in 1973, the
military coup, followed by seventeen years of the Pinochet dictatorship, and there followed a systematic campaign by the right wing

and the military to erase the past. A couple of generations of Chileans have lived in limbo, not knowing exactly what happened that Tuesday, September 11, 1973, not knowing who Salvador Allende was or what their country was like before the dictatorship. The collective memory had been brutally smothered. Chile needs to dig up its past in order to heal and mature.

In *Portrait in Sepia*, the section on the War of the Pacific, with Chile fighting against Peru and Bolivia, as seen from the perspective of Severo del Valle, constitutes one of the most moving parts of the novel. What personal experience did you live through as a result of that abominable war?

As you know I lived through the military coup in Chile of 1973. When violence and cruelty were unleashed, the terrified people asked themselves how it was possible for such a thing to happen in Chile, the most democratic and law-abiding country in South America. Well, our memory failed us. Those atrocities had happened before, during the revolution of 1891, when the armed forces rebelled and the country plunged into a bloodbath. During this period people were tortured, summarily executed, illegally arrested, taken in airplanes and thrown into the sea, the same as happened during the Pinochet dictatorship. During the revolution of 1891 more Chileans died in nine months than during the four years of the War of the Pacific. When a battle breaks out among relatives, my people turn into real barbarians. For this reason I wanted to write about the nineteenth century. I believe that during that battle-torn century to a large extent the Chilean character took shape: this explains many events that took place in the twentieth century.

Did you conceive the idea of a trilogy that includes *The House of the Spirits* with *Portrait in Sepia* or with *Daughter of Fortune*?

I had almost finished the first chapter of *Portrait in Sepia* when I realized that the main character could be a descendant of Eliza and Tao Chi'en, and in that way unite the two novels. Then I eliminated that first chapter and started to write a new novel, which would take place in San Francisco, with Aurora del Valle as their granddaughter; she would be taken in by Paulina.

Portrait in Sepia is like a bridge between The House of the Spirits and Daughter of Fortune. Which characters did you decide to take from one work to the other?

My readers told me they wanted to know more about these characters. I thought, well there seems to be something lacking in *Daughter of Fortune* because some of the characters were left hanging; this includes Tao Chi'en and Eliza Sommers. Nevertheless, as I was writing the novel *Portrait in Sepia* the one who developed into the most important character was Paulina del Valle.

I agree. Paulina first appears in Daughter of Fortune and develops further in Portrait in Sepia. Severo del Valle is depicted in Portrait as a young man in a more important role than in The House of the Spirits. Moreover, his acts carry more weight than those of the other characters. What future did you have in mind for him when you thought of him for the first time?

Twenty years ago Severo del Valle crossed my path when I wrote my first novel. In *The House of the Spirits* he is the father of Clara, Nívea's husband, the father of fifteen children, keen on politics. He has a secondary role in the story, and naturally, I never suspected that he would appear again in another book. When I had written forty pages of *Portrait in Sepia* I realized that Severo could be a substitute father for Aurora del Valle, by falling in love with the little girl's mother, Lynn. Naturally, Lynn could not remain in the book; therefore it was not a problem to take Severo back to Chile, into the arms of his first love, his cousin Nívea. Thus *Portrait in Sepia* became a bridge between my first and latest novels; this created a trilogy almost by chance. If this had been planned beforehand, I would have mentioned in *The House of the Spirits* that Severo del Valle only had one leg; he lost the other one during the War of the Pacific. Now I have an extra leg floating through the trilogy. I can assure you that more than one brainy professor will assume that I did it on purpose and that the miraculously reconstituted leg is a phallic symbol or an example of magic realism.

No doubt Severo del Valle is handsome, and Aurora del Valle seems to have always been in love with him.

When I wrote *The House of the Spirits* Severo del Valle was not an important character. He appears almost marginally, as Nívea's companion; this same feminist who had fifteen children, whose head is cut off in an accident, who tied herself to the door of the congressional building. The main character there is Nívea not Severo. He is almost a token, the father of all those children, and a kind of political aspirant.

In *Portrait in Sepia*, on the other hand, he has a very important role.

I did not have him very well delineated in my head when I wrote *The House of the Spirits*. But in this other novel, he emerged as one of the main characters. And as you noticed, I attributed things to this character in this other book that do not reappear in *The House of the Spirits*, such as the fact that he had only one leg.

Yes, I did notice that, and I did not imagine the two Severo del Valles to be physically alike. In *The House of the Spirits* he seemed fatter to me.

Well, he could have gotten fat as he grew older. Still at some point in *The House of the Spirits* I should have said that he had only one leg, and I would have if I had thought that some day I would write a novel like *Portrait in Sepia*, but of course I had not thought of it. These things all happened by chance.

What was Paulina del Valle's process of maturing and growth as she went from *Daughter of Fortune* to *Portrait in Sepia*?

Paulina del Valle is one of those characters who continue to grow on each page until they take control of everything. The model of this powerful woman, with unquenchable appetites and desires, sentimental, intelligent, and apt at business dealings, is my agent, the ineffable Carmen Balcells. For that reason the book is dedicated to her and to Tío Ramón, who was born on the same day as she was, and, like her, is one of those hyperbolic characters who one rarely encounters in this world. Both of them were born under the sign of Leo, and they have both been giants in my life. Paulina's role was originally to take Aurora to Chile, but she gained more and more importance to the point of becoming the main character.

Do you agree, as some critics say, that Paulina del Valle becomes dominant in the book?

Certainly, Paulina dominated me completely. She is one of those characters that command respect; you must let them do whatever they want because they know more than you do. It was no trouble at all for me to imagine her; I recall that I could smell her perfume in my house for months. I like Paulina del Valle, in spite of her arrogance and ostentation because she surprised me so many times. I did not expect her to marry her butler Fredrick Williams, or that she would pardon her husband's lover, Amanda Lowell. Naturally Paulina represents the upper class, the oligarchy, the political right wing in Chile, although this character has virtues that this kind of people rarely possess: astuteness, tolerance, curiosity, a cosmopolitan vision, sensuality, audacity, and initiative.

Which one is your favorite character in this novel? I think you identify with Nívea del Valle. Why?

My favorite character in this book certainly is Nívea del Valle, but it would be presumptuous of me to say that "I identify myself" with her. I like her personality, the strength of her decisions, the clarity with which she understands her destiny and how wisely she goes about solving problems, from those of love to raising her children as well as politics. I do not possess any of this clarity, unfortunately; I am under the impression that my destiny consists in blundering around and around in circles. I am impressed that Nívea was a feminist before the word was invented. In *The House of the Spirits* she would chain herself to the bars on the congressional building in order to demand the vote for women. She had many enemies because of her radical ideas, but she always had the admiration and support of her husband. When she dies by being decapitated in an automobile accident and her head rolls along the road and gets lost in the bushes, her enemies said: "Since she had lost her head while she was alive, there was no reason for her to keep it when she died." Of all the characters that have appeared in my books, Nívea is one of the few I would like to explore more in depth. Generally I wave goodbye to my characters when I finish a book, hoping they will not come back to bother me again, but I am not so lucky: many of them return disguised and with other names, but if I scrutinize them carefully they are recognizable. For example, Riad Halabí, the Turk in *Eva Luna* is very similar to Tao Chi'en in *Daughter of Fortune* and Fredrick Williams in *Portrait in Sepia*. Tránsito Soto and the Count of Satigny are like sister and brother to Amanda Lowell and Matías Rodríguez de Santa Cruz in *Portrait in Sepia*. Thus there are several who appear more than once.

Aren't you also a little bit contradictory like Nívea?

I recognize that she is a paradoxical character, liberal, feminist, a self-sacrificing mother, faithful wife; in fact all those characteristics do not suit the same person. I am also paradoxical in many ways. When I got married at twenty years of age, I refused to take my husband's last name. I was never known as Isabel Allende de Frías, as is customary in Chile. Nevertheless, I doted on Miguel like a geisha girl. I have been emancipated in many respects and am very conservative in others, such as everything related to honor, the family, housekeeping, and maternity. In these respects I have behaved like any lady from the time of my grandmother. Don't think that I am proud of that; on the contrary, it seems to me that it is pure nonsense that only now in my mature years, have I managed to shrug off a little bit. Nívea is complex and contradictory, like all really interesting people. I am pleased that she was a progressive woman for her time in political and social ideas, as well as in the development of her sexuality, but traditional in what relates to the family. Very few women of her time would have read the erotic books from the library and explored her own body to learn about pleasure and sensuality. Chile is a very Catholic country, where these things are sinful.

True, and Nívea was a freethinker from the waist up.

Regarding Nívea's fifteen children, think about the period, when there were no contraceptives; such a fertile woman as she was could have been pregnant all the time, considering how much she enjoyed going to bed with her husband.

Tell me about Aurora del Valle and love in her life. By the way, thank you for embellishing this book with passionate eroticism which unfortunately was not Aurora's lot in the same way.

For some reason that I can't explain, many of my main female characters suffer a frustrating first love. That is the case of Eva Luna, Eliza Sommers, Aurora del Valle and others, who fall in love with attractive, seductive, desperate or tragic men and, naturally it turns out bad for them. Later they find a second love that is more tranquil and safe, but the first love marks them forever. That has not happened to me at all. I married my first love, and we were happy for many years. For that reason I do not know why this theme is repeated in my books. It is not easy for me to write erotic stories, in spite of the many readers and critics, like you, who express the opinion that the love scenes in my books are not so bad. When writing about physical love one must follow a fine line that separates sensuality from vulgarity.

What affinities do you find in the development of the characters of Aurora and Eliza?

Affinities between these two? Aurora's character, in my opinion, is quite obscure. She is a person who has no memory of an important part of her life. It is through the discovery of what happened during those first years that she slowly develops an identity and strength. At first, she is a confusing character. Paulina and Eliza are much stronger; from the time they are sixteen years old they know exactly what they want to do.

First Mateo and later Eliza say to Aurora del Valle, "How lucky you are; you are not as beautiful as your mother." This is the only physical comment or evaluation that another character makes about her. Regarding herself, she speaks of her nightmares, little children in black pajamas, and declares that she was marked at birth with an invisible defect that she must overcome. In my opinion, the ending is somewhat ambiguous.

With regard to the characters?

Yes. The most convincing character in *Daughter of Fortune* is Tao Chi'en. There are many well-developed ones in *Portrait in Sepia*. Let's start with Severo del Valle, who is one of the good characters, and Mateo himself, who falls in with the bad ones; considering how detestable he is, still I consider him a man of exquisite refinement and absolute decadence, fin de siècle type. He sticks in the mind as a demoniac character. Then, I find Paulina outstanding. I also like Fredrick Williams very much. There is greatness about him, in spite of the fact that he tells of his humble origins and that his back is marked by the whipping he received for stealing a horse. He is capable of great loyalty. And above all, Nívea is a decent, brave, and imaginative person.

I think that almost all of them are subversive. There are characters like Lynn who are not strong; in my opinion, Lynn is a completely secondary character, and she appears in the book only to give birth to Aurora, and to start talking to Severo. I am interested in describing the strong characters: Nívea, Paulina, Eliza Sommers, Rose, then Clara, Blanca, Alba, in *The House of the Spirits*.

Clara ends up being strong in spite of the fact that she appears

to be absentminded, more involved in a spiritual world than in everyday life.

All of these characters have one thing in common: they do not accept what they are told; they rebel. They search for ways to escape from patriarchy, religion, the tremendous weight of tradition and the family. Some rebel through politics, or by being feminists, or finally participating as *guerrilleras*. Others like Clara rebel by evading reality completely in search of other worlds. Others like Paulina do it by taking the bull by the horns and confronting tradition directly, but she has the advantage of being born wealthy.

Consider the case of Aurora, in spite of the fact that her character seems obscure, incomplete because of the gap in her memory, she devotes herself to photography with such great passion!

Besides she does something at that time that no woman did: she left her husband. When she finds out about Diego's betrayal, she does not follow the advice given to her; she does not play dumb like most of the women of the time; instead she leaves.

Williams asks her to tell him the truth. And as soon as she tells him what happened, he advises her to postpone indefinitely her return to Caleufú. He tells her never to say she will not return, to just postpone it.

There was no divorce in Chile at that time, and there still is none.

I think that in the last analysis, every one of your strong characters reflects some facet of your personality. And with regard to Lynn, who dies young and beautiful, it seems that the very beautiful women like Rosa . . .

always die. (*They both laugh.*)

Why?

Because they are a pain. I can not save them. (*They keep on laughing.*)

They have to be killed! Who can live as high in the clouds as they do? On the other hand Nívea...

The character of Nívea is described several times, mousy but very resolute.

True. She was also very, very astute at sneaking into her uncle's library on the pretext of putting the prohibited volumes in order and reading them all. She also had the intuition to realize that Severo had been in love with Lynn.

But she never lost hope.

Is there a facet of Nívea that would have never occurred to you, and that sprang from her?

When Severo arrives, the last thing he expects is to run into Nívea at the port, and Nívea has gone to wait for him alone. There is a dialogue, and at one point he says to her, "I do not expect you to forgive me; I only hope you will forget me, Nívea. You deserve to be happy more than anyone else." She answers, "And who told you I want to be happy? That is the last adjective I would use to define what I want in the future. I want a life that is interesting, adventurous, different, passionate, in the final analysis almost anything but happy." That defined this character for me. From that moment Nívea started to grow in the novel because up to that point she had appeared very little. When she made such a statement that came from nowhere, I said to myself: Wow! This is the character I wanted to create.

Another detail that struck me from the first is that she goes alone. She appears during the nineteenth century around 1878 and shows up alone at the port determined to save him. And she is the one who finally persuades her uncle Vergara to pull him

out of the battlefield. Nívea saves his life in many ways, practical, spiritual, and psychic. When the doctors realize that his health is not improving, she decides to marry him. Going back to the trilogy, could it be made into a film as a continuous saga?

These three books can be read separately. In Spain the three will be published in December as a trilogy. If a television series could be produced, as you suggest, perhaps it would be necessary to give more unity to the whole series, because there is a certain lack of continuity among these three books.

Are you more pleased with your creation of *Portrait in Sepia* or *Daughter of Fortune*? First I would like your personal opinion and then the comments from your readers and critics.

It is difficult for me to judge the books I have written, even though every one has a place in my memory and my life, because I forget them. After I finish writing a book I move on to another project, and I don't read my earlier works again. I do not remember the details of any of them, especially not *The House of the Spirits* which I wrote twenty years ago. I am pleased with the way *Portrait in Sepia* turned out; I think it is a novel written with definite control of style in the way it is told which I have acquired during so many years of writing. Critics have been favorable, and it has sold well. I always say that it is not fair to compare the most recent novel with the others because it grows out of all the earlier ones, and there is a group of readers who are your fans. You can not compare the sales of the latest novel with one I wrote almost ten years ago when I was not so well known.

I understand. Let's return to *Portrait in Sepia*. Did you read much about this period in the history of Chile?

A great deal. Isn't it obvious?

Of course. It is curious how much you are in touch with Chilean customs, especially in the nineteenth century. Paulina tries in vain to keep her relatives from dropping by her house unan-

nounced, but they always do anyway, and she can not stop them. Chilean and Argentine relatives stop by for a visit whenever they please; that is part of the culture. And do you know who almost always sets the humorous tone? Paulina. Remember when her husband tries to pick her up, and she has gained so much weight he can not budge her, he says to her, "Shit, Paulina! Do you have lead in your panties?"

Paulina has many likeable things about her. For example, her husband's lover shows up, the lady she hated so much, Amanda Lowell, the one in the bed story. Remember when she appears again in Paulina's life?

Oh yes. Amanda.

At first Paulina is furious.

"What is this woman doing here!" she exclaims, but the two women end up on good terms.

Remember how much they had in common, especially Feliciano Rodríguez de Santa Cruz.

What is the theme of this book?

The theme of the book is memory. Aurora's entire development is an effort to fill the void in her mind of her first five years, which she does not manage to recall, but it makes her have terrible nightmares. She wants to know what happened, where she came from, who her father was. On finding out, she starts to define herself as a human being. Up to that moment she had been defined by others, especially her grandmother Paulina del Valle. Photography is the means she uses to explore her past and her subconscious, until at last her forgotten grandmother Eliza finally appears again. Eliza provides the answers to her questions. Thanks to Eliza she regains the memory of her beloved grandfather, Tao Ch'ien, who died tragically when she was only five years old. Finally she can relate her nightmares with her past and make sense out of her existence. At first she is an obscure character because she does not even know who she is, but as she comes to discover her true identity, her character is defined, and she becomes stronger and stronger in the novel.

I think I have a lot in common with her. I was raised without knowing who my father was, without ever hearing his name. I lived, like Aurora, surrounded by secrets, mysteries, forbidden topics that could not be mentioned, shameful affairs. Apparently my father committed misdeeds that no one would mention, and since I have a pathological imagination, I attributed crimes to him that were much worse than what the poor man actually did. Perhaps they were anatomically impossible sins! That is the way I was raised. In my search to decipher those mysteries, I ended up dedicating myself to writing. For her part, Aurora turns into a photographer in order to understand her past.

Do you think that with this book you have finished exploring the theme of memory?

Right now I am writing a long essay, actually a book, which *National Geographic* has asked me to write, also on the topic of memory. The idea came to life from a question someone from the audience asked me during a brief speech I gave at the opening of a conference of writers. The question was: "What is the role of nostalgia in your works?" I answered whatever struck my fancy at that moment, but I kept thinking about nostalgia and memory, about Aurora del Valle and the theme of *Portrait in Sepia*. One week later an editor for *National Geographic* called to ask me to write a book on this topic. He wanted to know the role Chile had in all this and I had to explain to him that I have lived less than half of my life in Chile, and when I visit there I feel like a foreigner because the truth is that my Chile is an invention and not a real country. It is a mythical Chile, the land described by Pablo Neruda.

That is what Unamuno always said. He did not believe in the history of Spain. He believed in the intra-history of Spain, a histo-

ry that is invisible and includes every person in it. The intra-history of Chile.

History is different for every person. For example, my recollections of the military coup are exactly the opposite of those of my best friend in Chile, Pía Leiva. She belongs to a family aligned to the right wing and lives in the country, in a very conservative environment. For her Allende was a demon, the same as Pinochet is a demon for me. Our versions of that period in history are completely opposite, polarized, but about the same reality.

Once I was asked in English what was Mendoza, Argentina; for me, I answered, "a state of mind." I think that nostalgia is precisely the detonator necessary to come face to face with the mood left clinging to a time long past. It is nostalgia, the remembrance of things past. It is your search for a time that is no longer yours.

It is also a time one invents.

In your case, precisely because you are a storyteller.

I have often said that with her mental power my grandmother moved the sugar bowl across the table. Honestly I am trying to remember if I ever saw it happen. Perhaps I never did, but we used to talk about it so much. There was so much discussion about the sugar bowl incident that it lives in my mind as if I had really seen it. But it is make-believe.

Those anecdotes and those visions become real as one hears them so often. Besides no one doubts their veracity. People do not what the bare facts; they prefer legends which are more alive and rich than simple facts. People reject documentation. Why document a story when fantasy and legends are more attractive? I used to have the bad habit of asking people, "Where did you get that from?"

We agreed that nostalgia plays an important role in your works. Tell me about Chile, which is an essential aspect of *Portrait in Sepia*.

It is the nostalgia of a legendary Chile, of a place to which I do not belong either. I was born in Lima. I went to Chile as a little girl. I lived there from when I was three until I was sixteen. Then we traveled with Tío Ramón. I returned to Chile when I was eighteen, but I had to leave because of the military coup, and I have never returned to live in Chile since. I have only lived there a few years. Nevertheless, Chile exerts such a powerful attraction for me, and my roots are so firmly planted there that it is my point of reference. I always return there when I write.

That past of yours as a wanderer, a gypsy, is what has made it possible for you to adapt to life in the United States better than some people who have lived here all their lives. It is true that you have created a world that is very sui generis. There are very few writers who have your need to never stop writing. "There is a place that comes to be when you arrive" says a love poem. There is a home that comes to be when you write.

Someone said that I had a town in my head.

Not just a town but rather a perpetually exuberant world.

Chronology

1942   Isabel Allende is born in Lima, Peru, where her father, Tomás Allende, first cousin of Salvador Allende, is a Chilean diplomat. Her mother, Francisca Llona, "doña Panchita," is the daughter of Isabel Barros Moreira and Agustín Llona Cuevas.

1945   Doña Panchita annuls her marriage to Tomás Allende and returns to Chile with her three small children to live in her father's home in Santiago, where the three children grow up under their mother's and grandfather's care.

1953–1958   Doña Panchita casts her lot with Ramón Huidobro, "Tío Ramón," a career diplomat assigned to Bolivia and Beirut. In Bolivia, Isabel attends a private North American school, and in Beirut, a private English school.

1958   Because of the Suez Canal crisis, Isabel returns to Chile to complete her secondary education. She meets her future husband, Miguel Frías, an engineering student.

1959–1965   Isabel works in Santiago for the FAO (Food and Agriculture Organization) of the United Nations.

1962   Isabel marries Miguel Frías.

1963   Her daughter, Paula, is born.

1964–1965   She travels through Europe; lives in Brussels and Switzerland with her husband and daughter.

1966   Returns to Chile, where her son, Nicolás, is born.

1967–1974   Writes for the magazine *Paula*. Forms part of the first editorial staff. Is responsible for the humor column *Los impertinentes*.

1973–1974 Collaborates on the children's magazine *Mampato*, in Santiago. Briefly directs *Mampato*. Publishes two stories for children, *La abuela Panchita* [Grandmother Panchita] and *Lauchas y lauchones*, and a collection of articles, *Civilice a su troglodita* [Civilize Your Troglodyte].

1970   Salvador Allende is elected the first socialist president of Chile. Isabel's stepfather, Ramón Huidobro, is named ambassador to Argentina.

1970–1975 Isabel works on Santiago television Channels 13 and 7; she hosts a comedy program and an interview show. Both are very popular.

1973   Her play *El embajador* is performed in Santiago. Coup d'etat, September 11, led by General Augusto Pinochet Ugarte. Salvador Allende dies; assassination is suspected. The military government reports suicide.

1975   Isabel and family move to Venezuela. Because of the threat of the dictatorship in Chile, they remain there for thirteen years. She works for *El Nacional*, a Caracas newspaper.

1978   Temporary separation from Miguel Frías. For two months she lives in Spain.

1979–1982 She works as administrator at the Colegio Marroco, a secondary school in Caracas.

1981   When she receives news that her ninety-nine-year-old grandfather is dying, she begins to write him a letter that will become the manuscript of *The House of the Spirits*.

1982   Publishes *La casa de los espíritus*, Plaza y Janés, Barcelona.

1984   Alfaguara, in Madrid, publishes *La gorda de porcelana* [The Voluptuous Porcelain Figure], a brief, humorous novel written in 1974 and submitted to the publisher in 1975. Publishes *Of Love and Shadows*, Plaza y Janés.

1985   English translation of *The House of the Spirits*, Alfred A. Knopf, translation by Magda Bogin.

1987	Divorces Miguel Frías. Publication of *Eva Luna*, Plaza y Janés; Knopf publishes English version by Margaret Sayers Peden, who will provide English translations of subsequent works. First meeting with Willie Gordon in San Jose, California.
1988	Marries Willie Gordon in San Francisco, July 7. They make their home in San Rafael, California.
1989	Publishes *Cuentos de Eva Luna*, Plaza y Janés.
1990	Democracy is restored in Chile. Patricio Aylwin is elected president. Isabel returns after a fifteen-year absence to accept the Gabriela Mistral prize from the hands of the president.
1991	Publication of *The Stories of Eva Luna*. December 6, in Madrid, Paula suffers an attack of porfiria and falls into a coma as Isabel is launching *El Plan Infinito,* published by Plaza y Janés.
1992	Paula dies in San Rafael, December 6, in Isabel and Willie's home.
1993	English version of *The Infinite Plan.* In August, *The House of the Spirits* is staged in London. October 22, premiere of the film version of *The House of the Spirits* in Munich, produced by Bernd Eichinger and directed by Billie August, with the following cast: Winona Ryder, Vanessa Redgrave, Meryl Streep, Glenn Close, Jeremy Irons, and Antonio Banderas.
1994	*Paula* is published in Spanish by Plaza y Janés; in German and Dutch, with the subtitle "novel"; and in English. Film version of *De amor y de sombra,* directed by Betty Kaplan and starring Antonio Banderas.
1997	*Afrodita*, Plaza y Janés.
1998	*Aphrodite* is published in Italian in January and in English in March. Isabel is honored with the Dorothy and Lillian Gish Prize for having "contributed to the beauty of the world." The $200,000 prize is awarded in a ceremony in New York, crowning a long list of international prizes in her career.

1998   *Hija de la fortuna,* first published in Spanish, Plaza y
          Janés.
1999   *Daughter of Fortune,* published in English, Harper y
          Collins.
2000   *Retrato en Sepia,* published in Spanish, Plaza y Janés.
2001   *Portrait in Sepia,* published in English, HarperCollins.
2002   *La ciudad de las bestias,* first part of a trilogy of adven-
          tures for teenagers, to be published in October.

Notes

Introduction

In the mid-seventies, in exile in Venezuela, the two Chilean families were reunited in the same apartment building: Isabel, her husband Miguel, her children Paula and Nicolás on one floor; Panchita and Tío Ramón on another. When Panchita read *La casa de los espíritus* [*The House of the Spirits*] the first time, she realized that a great work had been born. There was material there for three novels, not just one. After unsuccessfully attempting to interest Venezuelan publishers in the book, Panchita wrote editor Javier Vergara in Buenos Aires; he and his wife had been friends of hers for many years. They rejected the novel but recommended Carmen Balcells' literary agency in Barcelona. The Argentine writer and journalist Tomás Eloy Martínez later gave them the agency's address. "We looked for a *chasquí*, which is what I call a messenger," Panchita recounts, "to take the manuscript to Spain, because between us, Isabel and I couldn't put together enough money to send it by mail." Then Isabel had the inspired idea of calling Carmen from Caracas. The publication of the novel, in 1982, was so successful that it easily covered the shipping costs for that first manuscript and for all the manuscripts to come.

Isabel refuses to accept prevailing dogmas, a trait developed at an early age. In her secondary school, La Maisonette, she received the highest grade in her religion class exam—a course taught by Marta Cruz-Coke, a Chilean intellectual and director of museums, archives, and libraries in Chile—at a time she declared she had no faith. Marta Cruz-Coke commented, as she told the story to me in the office of the director of the National Library of Chile, a beautiful nineteenth-century building, sitting before the Toribio Medina painting that covers most of the wall, "But, in fact, Isabel's entire life is a single act of faith." When I asked her what Isabel was like as a girl, Marta answered: "She wasn't pretty, but when she smiled her whole face lit up."

Rebellions and Challenges

It was Pablo Neruda who advised Isabel to collect her humorous articles and publish them in book form, which is what she did. In July of 1974, nearly a year after the death of that poet, the Lord Cochrane publishing house printed an edition of ten thousand copies of *Civilice a su troglodita* [Civilize Your Troglodyte], selections from Isabel Allende's humor column for the magazine *Paula*, with illustrations by Ricardo Güiraldes. That year, too, for the Zapatito Roto division of the same house, she published two books for children: *Lauchas y lauchones, ratas y ratones* [Mouslets and Mice, Ratlets and Rats] and *La abuela Panchita* [Grandmother Panchita], the latter with puppet illustrations by Marta Carrasco. Grandmother Panchita, as the name indicates, is none other than Isabel's mother, Doña Panchita. Juanita, the protagonist of the first story, "*Juanita en el campo*" [Juanita in the Country], is undoubtedly Paula, just as Perico, in "*Perico busca un amigo*" [Perico Looks for a Friend] is Nicolás, Paula's younger brother, who today is living in California with his three small children. The stories are dedicated to Isabel's children, Paula and Nicolás, and were published when they were eight and five, respectively. For Isabel, spinning these stories was everyday work. In *Paula*, she tells her daughter, "Nicolás and you grew up listening to Granny's English songs and my stories. Every night when we tucked you into bed, you gave me a subject or a first sentence, and in three seconds I would create a made-to-order story. Since then I have lost the knack for instant inspiration, but I hope it isn't dead and that in the future my grandchildren will revive it." From her brothers to her children and grandchildren, three generations of children have marveled at Isabel Allende's stories.

In 1983, Alfaguara of Madrid published her allegory, *La gorda de porcelana* [The Voluptuous Porcelain Figure], a little book with delicious illustrations by Fernando Krahn. In this deceptively simple story, one sees Isabel's distinctive imagination at work, creating a fable about boredom and the redemptive power of fantasy. It is the story of a timid notary who sees a seductive statue in the window of an antique shop, a voluptuous female porcelain, scantily veiled and holding grapes and doves in her hands. Don Cornelio represents the monotony of a mechanical, bourgeois life until the magic of the statue provides an unexpected twist to his gray existence. Seized by a strange urgency when he first sees the statue in the shop window, Don Cornelio spends his entire month's salary, which is everything he has, to acquire it. The sensual porcelain comes to life to turn Don Cornelio around and point him toward an unexpected fate. The man wonders about the statue's purpose: "Obviously, it was not designed to be a lamp, or to stand in the vestibule to hang overcoats on, and no one had used it as adornment anywhere, for it took up more space than a bicycle and was as fragile as a good intention." Using humor and elegance, the story transcends the anecdotal to an intimate desire to live a more authentic life. The truth is that Isabel is Don Cornelio, and the lush lady is fantasy. Isabel left this story at the reception desk of the publishing house in 1978 when she was living in Madrid, separated from her husband. The story reached the desk of the editor of children's books, Michi Strausfeld, who tried in vain to locate the author. Isabel had gone back to Caracas to rejoin her family, leaving no address. Michi Strausfeld waited patiently, sure that sooner or later she would have word from the author of the story, and in 1982, when Isabel Allende returned to Madrid to launch *The House of the Spirits,* she immediately got in touch with her. It was Michi Strausfeld who published the story in 1983 and who convinced the German publisher Suhrkamp that an interesting novelist had been born. From then on, Suhrkamp Verlag has published all of Isabel Allende's books in German, with unprecedented success. *La gorda de porcelana*, in contrast, has never been republished or translated, because Isabel was never happy with it.

Isabel was also well known for her humor column in *Paula*, a magazine founded by Delia Vergara in 1967. "This first feminist publication shook the provincial stupor in which we were vegetating." The magazine was founded with a subsidy from a somewhat eccentric millionaire who had no ideological platform, though Delia Vergara used the forum to promote her feminist ideas. Isabel Allende, a resolute young woman whose most valuable credentials were her incorruptible humor and her talent, joined a team of professional journalists at the magazine and wrote a column entitled *Los impertinentes*. "My lack of credentials was embarrassing," Isabel Allende wrote in *Paula* with her usual frankness. "I had a head filled with fantasies, and [as a result of my nomadic school days] my writing was peppered with errors. In spite of all that, Delia Vergara offered me a feature page with no conditions other than it be ironic, because in the midst of so many argumentative articles, she wanted something light. I accepted, without any idea of how difficult it is to be funny on demand."

Isabel's theatrical works produced in Chile—*El embajador* [The Ambassador] in 1971; *La Balada del medio pelo* [Ballad of a Nobody], 1973; and *Los siete espejos* [Seven Mirrors], 1974—delineate with laughter and tears the author's social conscience. Beginning with *The House of the Spirits* (and excepting only *Aphrodite*), all of Isabel's works exhibit an undeniable social commitment.